The Magic

THE STORY OF TC
ST IVES AND A ⌐⌐

Eunice Campbell

WITH CONTRIBUTIONS FROM

Wilhemina Barns-Graham
Sven Berlin
Ian Breakwell
Terry Frost
Michael Miller
Martha Patrick
Keith Richardson-Jones
Eve el Salahi
and
Prof. Lionel Haward

redcliffe

First published in 1994
by Redcliffe Press Ltd.,
22 Canynge Square, Bristol

© Eunice Campbell and contributors

ISBN 1 872971 78 4

British Library Cataloguing in Publication Data
A catalogue record for this book is available from
the British Library.

Typeset by Mayhew Typesetting, Rhayader, Powys
Printed in Great Britain by The Longdunn Press, Bristol

Contents

Tom Early: portrait by Denis Mitchell   iv

Dedication   v

Acknowledgements   vi

The window of the eye *Sven Berlin*   7

How find you now, Tom Early? *Sven Berlin*   12

Tom Early 1914–1967 *Eunice Campbell*   14

The river of art and the sea of the
unconscious *Michael Miller*   52

A portrait done from memory *Ian Breakwell*   55

More private views   57

Some public views   61

Notes on a sheaf of poems by Tom Early
Sven Berlin   64

A voyage to Japan *Tom Early*   65

Illustrations

The text is illustrated with black & white reproductions
of paintings by Tom Early on pages 48 to 51 and 79,
and with colour plates between pages 32 and 33.

Tom Early: portrait by Denis Mitchell. Oil, 1947.

I dedicate this book to my husband, Tom Early, who 'opened my eyes' to those things that really matter in this life.

And to Denis Mitchell, his painting partner, who became too ill to make the contribution he wanted for this book, but who contributed in the best way anyone can to the richness of another's life by the wealth of a long, true and lasting friendship.

ACKNOWLEDGEMENTS

Without Sven Berlin, this book would not have been written. I owe everything to his unceasing encouragement, generosity of heart, and ever present belief in the 'rightness' of the venture. I am grateful beyond measure to him, and for his astounding recollection of Tom after a gap of 40 years.

I am also immensely indebted to Sothebys for the beautiful 'gratis' photography, and to Mark Adams of the Modern British Pictures Department in particular for his sensitive and enthusiastic response to Tom's work. Through him came the unexpectedly generous offer of help in producing the illustrations.

I thank Irving Grose for his interest and encouragement, and for staging a beautiful exhibition of Tom's work at the Belgrave Gallery, London. To Michael Tooby and Carolyn Trevivian at the Tate Gallery, St Ives, my special thanks for their keen interest at a vital moment, and to David and Tina Wilkinson of the Book Gallery, St Ives who responded so immediately to Tom's work, my gratitude indeed.

Those others who have contributed from an artistic point of view, as well as with personal remembrances, will surely know how much I value their particular additions to this book.

And, finally, my special thanks go to all those friends and relatives who, after so long a period of time, have nonetheless whole-heartedly given their recollections of Tom and whose names, where not specifically mentioned, I would now like to acknowledge. They are Mr Peter Early, Mr Francis Early, Mrs Anne Early Attewell, Miss Marion Banks, Mrs Catherine Crawford, Mrs Barbara Hart, the Revd Maurice Kidd, Miss Mary Phillips, Miss Alison Butcher, Mr and Mrs Q. Beattie, Mr and Mrs J. Connor, Miss Fanny Moretti, Mr and Mrs J. Moss, Mr and Mrs Denis Cartwright, Mrs Barbara Molland, Mrs Barbara Luttrell, Mr Derek Barnett, Fraulein Dorothea Hollweg, Mrs Jane Mitchell and Mr David Ainley. Others will know how greatly I appreciate their continued concern and unrecorded promptings.

The window of the eye

It is the unexpected concomitance of two events that brings about the illumination of one, or the understanding of both, where before there was darkness.

Often I find it difficult to write about another artist because the narrowness of my own lane of vision fences me from his visual perception, so that I cannot always see what he is up to; or not understand if I can see, especially if I am working.

When I received the letter asking me to write an article about Tom Early I was struck dumb: first because I didn't know how I should write it; second because he was exactly the answer I was looking for to solve a problem before me. I was struggling to describe, in poetic form, what it is that brings about the poetic image, which in the end is what the painter paints. Not because I had been asked: I simply wanted to know. I have always wanted to know, because nobody does know. It is one of those unexplained things. No one is sure about hemicephalic headaches, or epilepsy, the falling sickness. I had got so far:

> There is a special device
> Planted behind the face
> That detects gold:
> It is triggered apace
> If you look each way twice
> To behold
> Something simultaneously
> Inside and out,
> Like throwing a stone
> (If thou durst)
> Through the window of the eye
> On the threshold of sight –
> Give a sudden shout,
> Flash a bright light,
> Or the equivalent –
> Like a flea leaps Eternity –
> (Unexpectedly, as if sent)
> And then there is a silent
> Explosion – the image is there.

That is as far as I had got when the letter came from Tom Early's widow, Eunice Campbell, who at my suggestion was writing a book about him:

'Would you be willing to add your remembrances – particularly of him as an artist?' It fitted exactly. After 45 years his frail figure rose before me like a ghost to tell me what I was trying so unsuccessfully to say, and immediately became part of my struggle to say it.

The year I met him I wrote about his work in Denys Val Baker's *Cornish Review*: 'a unique painter who leads us through landscapes of terrifying loneliness without ever seeming to be aware of our dismay and our wonder at walking within a dream he has made.' Tom Cross, in *Painting the Warmth of the Sun*, writes of Tom Early's painting of *Tuckingmill Chapel* as 'having a feeling of the "great wind" which surged through the souls of early Methodist preachers while they held their audiences in terror of hell fire trembling before the heavenly host' – which is quite as profound as any remark I have made and made 30 years after Tom Early was painting in St Ives. He was there long enough to become part of the whole hurricane at its centre, had shows at the Castle Inn and was a member of the Penwith Society at its inception. But his work was left out of the great 1985 St Ives Exhibition at the London Tate, in which I was gratuitously represented by one sculpture and one drawing. But never mind all that. Tom Cross's remarks and my own have kept his name alive, and strangely enough, both point to a cosmic terror and loneliness; also, in our different ways, to the Unconscious Mind of Man.

One might imagine from this that Tom Early was a rough, violent person who instilled fear into people – as myself for some reason. Not at all. He was a quiet fragile man and as suitably dressed in a blue lounge suit as any young country doctor visiting his patients; saying very little, as though perhaps he was diagnosing the invisible part of the world around him, with a special glass stethoscope, listening to the human heart, the beat of a seashell, a hill or a ruined mineshaft. As with Magritte, who dressed like a bank manager, he was quite conventional, wore glasses and no one would have dreamed he painted those outstanding pictures. The skin on his face was curiously scarred as though he had been burned at some time and had plastic surgery. But myself having just come out of a hideous war as Forward Observer for the Royal Artillery, I was used to such things and observant of them, even when, as in Tom's case, they were not in anyway disfiguring.

Sometimes of a winter evening I would have a drink with him in the Sloop and talk when it was quiet, but he was not a great drinker and I believe he limited himself to half-pints – not like the Gargantuan drink-ups there used to be when Sydney Graham and I met up with each other if a painting or a poem had been sold. Tom Early would not have wanted that, though he may have smiled to watch it and cared about the wave of poetry that poured through us. He was the Quiet Man; the Special Man to whom we were drawn because he painted pictures of Old Testament power and constructed their curious lunar architecture with incandescent light that made me think he had some particular device fitted behind his high frontal bone that put him in touch with a cosmic age that had burnt itself out some centuries before I met him – the sombre colours: 'olive greens, greys, Naples yellow, Antwerp blue', as he described them; with sometimes a scar of pure vermilion as if he had cut the surface of the eye while painting. No, he was not a man of violence, but, like all good artists, he had a pent-up energy in him, which, if not used in creation would destroy him; yet without a perfect mechanism to direct it.

It was in no way a shock when on one occasion of a wet winter evening when we left the Sloop, on our way to see his paintings at the Castle Inn, run by Endell Mitchell, a close friend of mine and brother to sculptor Denis Mitchell, that he suddenly faltered beside me and fell; I realised immediately that it was an epileptic fit, having come upon it quite recently in the Army when a young soldier on guard with me went down. So I was able to be helpful to my friend now and did not panic. Fortunately it was *un petit mal*, which was over quite soon and if anyone noticed they would have only thought I was helping a friend with too much to drink. His face was slightly cut: I remember seeing his smooth fragile skin glistening in the rain which had been torn at other times. His glasses had fallen off and looked like a lunar insect that had just bitten him in the face.

I saw him partly home until he said he was all right to go alone the rest of the way. I think it was Carbis Bay where I visited him a day or two later, and remember him smiling as if pleased I had come. He had elastoplast, not on his face but hinging his glasses, and also round the edge of his improvised palette which I thought was made of glass; it was certainly transparent and I wondered if it was a way of getting light to shine in from behind. He was so totally original that it is something he might have considered.

By now the whole pattern had come together and I realised why, as a young doctor, he was unable to practise any more.

Denis Mitchell was his friend also and used to take Tom out on the motorbike. One day at St Just they stopped by a particular clifftop formation that Tom wanted to look at.

'He seemed to have no fear at all,' said Denis. 'He climbed on a narrow ledge so that he could have a good look round with a sheer drop of 300 feet to the rocks below. And there I was quaking: 'What if he has an epileptic fit out there?' I thought. 'I shall have to get an ambulance and fire brigade to rescue him, if he isn't already smashed to pieces on the rocks.'

His work in the Castle was impressive because it was completely unique in its *firstness*: he wasn't trying to paint like John Park or Ben Nicholson as most of the artists were – he was painting like Tom Early. He had a natural primitiveness: not like Alfred Wallis, because Wallis painted with innocence 'what used to be', the tools and setting, the sea and landscape of his trade – 'guessed it all.' Tom Early painted the images before him but at the same time looking inwardly behind the face and including the images of the mind; the hills and valleys of the unconscious; so that an engine-house became like an ancient temple seen on the road to Damascus, and a mine shaft like a shaft tomb in old Mycenae or the tunnel graves of County Meath. He was concomitant to Wallis but not *of* him. He was a natural poet: Wallis was a simple realist. Tom Early created the poetic image within and outside himself, with its accompanying emotions.

I don't think his paintings were records of a psychosis or diagrams of a psychotic experience or that his fits were the cause of his doing them, even though that may have weakened the dykes that keep in the ocean of the unconscious which is vital to the artist of our time from flooding day-to-day life. But I do think he was presented to us as an archetype of the kind of experience that happens to artists down the ages – not as a psychosis, but as the action of the mind at the deeper levels of the unconscious, as distinct from the brain with its machine for logic, by presenting the inner and outer images in a silent explosion that makes them one: that is the creative act and charges the pigment with a light of its own.

Although I have no medical knowledge I would venture to say that the fits were due to the malfunctioning of the brain because it was not fitted with that special device (like an overdrive) that can deal with the enormous charge of energy that takes place in the mind when a painting comes into being: the magic device with which nearly every great artist has been fitted. Without which malfunctions occur and you get the madness of Kit Smart, John Clare, Van Gogh, usually ending in suicide. It can kill or create. For the Special, the Beautiful People to whom Tom Early belonged, life was tragic: for him, not because of his gift, but because the machinery that went with it was faulty.

I believe Tom Early was well aware of his destiny and what was happening to him. As a doctor he was aware of the importance of the unconscious and believed that all the arts were not separate but part of a network of rivers that were all flowing into one ocean which was the Unconscious. As with John Keats, who also had a medical training, he knew the dangers: Keats to wait for the moment when he must spew up his own lungs – 'become spectre thin and die' – Tom Early to expect an invisible tiger to leap on his back and strike him down. Yet neither man flinched. For those who think art is an infantile game that should not be taken too seriously, I here pronounce it a game of life and death from which the faint hearted intellectual should hide in his mother's skirts.

For all that, Eunice Campbell has told me that he was not killed by his malady of falling sickness, but, ironically, he fell down a deep hole in the dark and broke his leg, which later brought him to the final areas of destruction, as if even the Gods were jealous of the magic he was entrusted to interpret for each of us who would think life is worth extending into something fine and strange, no matter how difficult the ways of doing so have become.

I think it is for us to add our strength to the courage of his widow to preserve the name and work of this artist who showed each of us (without he himself knowing) that the only way to paint is out of your own vision no matter how narrow it might be or by what impediment it might be saddled; even to produce images 'seen through the wrong end of a telescope' with, as Early says 'human and animal forms which I perhaps see only briefly in clouds, trees and houses, so that often the finished painting does not bear a strict resemblance to the scene'.

I am convinced that Peter Lanyon, who first introduced Tom Early to me in 1946 and was very excited by his paintings – Bryan Wynter also – saw, through him, what to do with their Cornwall that was in them. It is to be hoped that the Tate will this time find a place in their New Temple of Art at St Ives for this unique painter who painted the poetic image from both sides of the window of the eye, there to give light and understanding where before was darkness.

SVEN BERLIN

11

How find you now, Tom Early?

How find you now, Tom Early,
Since you walked the Abyss
On a thread no thicker than a thought,
Stretched from pole to pole
Against the stars, and the jellyfish moon
Stung you with fire:
Insect spectacles bit your face
Like giant dragonflies,
And you remained articulate and whole.
Man of the Eyes: but vanished into space.

Nothing could keep
You from making new land
Out of terror and loneliness
Of which none of us can stand the stress –
And not weep.

How find now your hand?

The snowdrops in their silences
Have told the goldfinch and the hare
That you were there transforming the hills,
Orchestrating the sunset,
Watched by the sacred fox that kills
From the rocks near his earth,
And calls in the blue frost
Till his mate gives birth.

How forget you – at what cost?

You talked of the deep ocean
Of the mind and how
All man's art, by one motion,
Flows from the hills every hour
Into one soul, one heart, one emotion:

But we had you lost.

Dear Tom! Not fate but those in awe
And love who saw
You of late at the last door

With that simple smile
Knew they must wait awhile
To gather your fallen dream.
Nothing to do with luck
But your indifference to all fear
When the Tiger struck, makes you so dear,
So sweet a soul to meet –
As rare as radium in Oxford Street.

As with Dante in Hell
With his one love, you reached up and rang
The Poetry Bell, till the angels sang;
And took your offering alone
To the altar stone
Where Beauty bowed!

I found you there.

Farewell, Tom Early! Fare you well!
Thou art an angel unsung
And I could not tell.

SVEN BERLIN

Tom Early: 1914–1967

Beginnings in St. Ives

It was an accident that brought my husband, Tom Early, into painting. Following a horrible physical mishap he had gone to Cornwall to convalesce at his widowed mother's home in its superlatively beautiful position high up on the cliffs above Carbis Bay, and overlooking the great sweep of St. Ives Bay. Someone had given him a box of paints 'to fill in the time', and so began a whole new creative experience for a man who already passionately loved the arts and most particularly music and literature.

It is now more than 25 years since Tom's death, and, because a quarter of a century is a kind of landmark, I found myself quite unexpectedly responding when, at just that crucial time, the suggestion to 'write a book' was put to me by Sven Berlin.

For many years I have cherished the hope that Tom might be accorded recognition in the world of art – albeit of a modest cameo kind – because it is a world to which he most truly belongs, and this if only because he was a man of totally original vision. In a relatively short painting life the pictures he created made a contribution of a quite unique kind, and it was this quality which, no doubt, was instantly recognised by his near neighbour in Carbis Bay, Ben Nicholson. Ben then kept his motor-cycle in Tom's mother's garage, and so came upon his first efforts. He encouraged him to continue, and thus began in 1946 Tom's active painting life. Although the endorsement was of great importance I suspect that the inner flame was already very well ignited, and not by any means to be extinguished.

Just at this time the activities of the artists' community in St. Ives were beginning to run into some schism, and all this has been well documented elsewhere. All I need say here is that, out of his natural enthusiasms and the encouragement he was receiving, Tom began to enter more fully into the artists' fraternity, and was soon actually exhibiting.

He had come to know Denis Mitchell, with whom he had attended a few basic painting classes in 1947, and together they went out on Denis's motorbike to paint and sketch the local land and seascapes. Sven Berlin in his Tribute mentions Denis's recollection of Tom once treading on quite dangerous ground in order to have a good look around, but such was his total absence of any kind of fear regarding his illness, and so absorbed was he at that and any other such moment, it just never occurred to him that he might sustain a fatal fall. Some may have felt this was a kind of

14

recklessness, but I believe it was a self-obliterating response to intense matters of moment and to those around him.

One day Tom wanted to paint the fascinating face of an old tramp he had casually met, and so he took him back to the Carbis Bay house. Later he got into tremendous hot water for entertaining the old man to tea in his mother's drawing-room, but for Tom this would have been an entirely natural thing to do, and the mixture of scruff and refinement was irrelevant. Once, in 1950/51 when he was making sketches for his St. Paul's paintings, he went high up into a bombed and potentially dangerous building opposite the great church, and, on being spotted by a vigilant London 'Bobbie', was promptly and somewhat unceremoniously hauled down.

There is no doubt that his courage in the face of potentially lethal grand-mal epilepsy was extraordinary. The reference Sven makes to his facial scarring was the result of a fall into a fire during a seizure earlier in 1946 in Leeds, but, as with every set-back, he never allowed such 'interruptions' to interfere with the pursuit of life. He faced and embraced life to the full and, in the main, rejoiced in it.

This is not to say that he never had his moments of despair and depression; indeed, at one stage, suicide had not been far from his mind. This was during those early painting years in Cornwall when both he and his mother were quite certainly each experiencing frustrations of a peculiar kind, and he finding little hope then of breaking free from them.

Tom's first marriage to a Czech doctor in 1944 had begun to break up after only two or three years, and this, coupled with the inevitable problems of suddenly living under the same roof with his kind but sternly disciplined Cornish methodist parent, must sometimes have put him under almost intolerable strain.

He survived this, however: no doubt because he was at last beginning to externalise for the first time through paint those profound emotions, visions and needs which, until then, had been mainly met through music and literature.

At this time exhibitions for those artists in the 'modern' faction in St. Ives were held in Downing's Bookshop and the Castle Inn, and Tom and Denis had a first show together at the Castle Inn in September 1947, another in July 1948, and at Downing's Bookshop in July 1949. They had also exhibited in Percy Lake's Book and Paper Shop in Tregenna Place, where Percy had an upstairs room set aside for such events. In June 1949 the first exhibition of the Penwith Society was held in the rented and subsequently transformed St. Ives Public Hall in Fore Street, and Tom's work was well featured in this. In 1950 he was elected to the Penwith Society of Arts. On July 11th, 1951 he had rather amusingly written

15

about a possible picture sale from the Castle Inn: 'About the picture, I went in to the Castle last week and found it was one of the few paintings I've done which I really like! So I put a stiff price on it (£15!) in the hopes of discouraging the chap, who wasn't there, but I don't know if he's bought it. Damn these people, why can't they go for the ones one doesn't like oneself?!'

It is well reported that he seemed never to be unduly affected by the tensions and often fiercely varying attitudes arising out of the formation of the new Society, and that he allowed most of the surging passions to ride over him. But this is not to say that he had no clear ideas of his own about things, as later expressed in a letter of March 17th, 1951. He had said he would sponsor a prospective exhibitor for the next Penwith exhibition. 'He (the artist) brought two pictures in gouache, which I thought were absolutely grand — in fact, if they reject them I think I shall resign in protest!' They were, in fact, rejected, as Tom shortly afterwards explodes: 'Blast these Penwith people, they've gone and chucked out the pictures, making some fatuous remarks about being very good as illustration etc. etc.' He did not, however, resign. In all this I believe he simply never permitted his own 'core being' to be ultimately disturbed. The issue would surely have had to be one of overwhelming significance.

During this time he was exposed to the work of, and involved with, Peter Lanyon (to whom he was distantly related), Terry Frost, Wilhelmina Barns-Graham, John Wells, Sven Berlin and all those others whose names now shine out of that dynamically creative era. In the midst of it Tom's work remained fresh and unaffected, reflecting the essence of the man himself. It could, no doubt, be said that he was sometimes influenced at a subtle level by those working so powerfully around him, but his own distinctive style was never so overlaid or lost that it was not instantly recognisable. He was always true to his own Self, and, as he writes in a letter of April 10th, 1951, '. . . with Art I believe that one has just got to let come out what will from deep inside one . . . if it won't that's just too bad, but there's nothing much one can do about it!' and 'seriously, one has to put down what one must, or bust, might be a good motto for an artist of whatever calling! Often I have found that I have painted a picture, and about two or three months later see something in it which had completely escaped me. Which tends to make me sympathetic towards mysticism!'

With reference to an assertion that he 'is lazy' and 'getting influenced by the Ben Nick crowd' he states quite simply to the first 'I am' and rather more emphatically to the second 'I am not'. As Picasso said, 'It is not what an artist does that counts — but what he is.'

In February 1949 Tom wrote for Paul Hodin about his painting and attitudes generally to the arts, and a similar piece in the same month for Denys Val Baker:

1. I started painting at the end of 1946; an illness had forced me to give up practising medicine, and living near St Ives in Cornwall it was natural to try painting. The first few small water colours were nothing out of the ordinary. But I was curious to try my hand at oil painting and other techniques, I was encouraged by friends, so I went on. First on paper, then on wood and canvas, I found I enjoyed painting with oils very much. There is a pub in St. Ives which shows paintings throughout the year, and with a friend I had my first exhibition here, in September 1947. In July 1948 we again showed in St. Ives.

2. So far most of my painting has been done in this westmost end of Cornwall, where the light and colours are always changing. But what attracts me even more is the variety of *Form*, both natural and man-made. Sea, cliffs, clouds; tin-mines, of which there are hundreds scattered around in various states of decay, and the huge china-clay dumps near St. Austell which form a landscape like that of the moon seen through a telescope. These are just a few examples out of thousands. Any scene which has mystery appeals to me; such as the pattern of smoke and chimneys looking over Halifax and other West Riding towns, or in London the dishevelled old brewery near the shot-tower, crowned by its red lion. But the actual scene is only the beginning, and usually my imagination runs riot and adds human – or animal-like – forms which I perhaps see only briefly in clouds, trees, houses etc. So that often the finished painting does not bear a strict resemblance to the scene.

3. *Colour* is difficult to separate from form – the two overlap so often, one suggesting the other. I think I find the more sombre colours (olive green, greys, Naples yellow, Antwerp blue) more satisfying than brighter colours. Cornwall has stimulated this preference, for much of the country away from the coast has a rather sombre look during winter and early spring. But I enjoy searching for the right place in a painting to put the suggestion of orange, emerald green or other bright colours.

4. *Supports, grounds etc.* I enjoy painting on wood very much, in spite of its dangers, mainly because different grains give one so many different surfaces to work on. Besides, I like if possible to carry a picture right through from the beginning (planing and sizing the wood) to the end (framing). Another technique which

I like using is Indian ink with water colours or even poster colours, which on paper or cardboard prepared suitably give an effect rather like that of gouache.

5. *Other arts.* I was devoted to other arts (music, poetry, the novel) before I became interested deeply in painting. I think the importance of different arts influencing one another is mainly subconscious, though of course this can happen on conscious levels as well (e.g. John Piper's designs for the opera 'Simone Boccanegra' at Sadler's Wells, how they heightened the already powerful emotional effect of the music). But I think that most conscious attempts to mingle two or more arts are likely to fail, such as the 'colour organ', Disney's film 'Fantasia' etc. Perhaps the best simile is that of several rivers all flowing into the same sea, which is the unconscious.

In a letter dated February 21st, 1951 Tom writes, '. . . it is now 8 months since I last did an oil (Cape Cornwall). I painted a few water colours when I was in London in October, but apart from framing them and photographing others, nothing. All the *passion* which has to be there when I want to paint seems to have left me for the time. I only hope it will come back!'

Then, writing on March 17th, he excitedly says, 'Rejoice with me – my lazy fit of non-painting has gone (for the time being, anyhow!). I'll tell you how it happened. Do you ever see the 'Observer' on Sunday? Last Sunday there was a lovely photo. on p. 1. which I saw at once was just asking to be painted. So I started off on a piece of hardboard, 30" × 30" which I had prepared 6 months ago (Ye Gods, *6 months*!) with oils. Then last week I was over at Peter Lanyon's taking some colour photos. of his big painting for London – about 9 × 4 feet – (I earned £1 there!) – when he told me about painting on paper with gouache then, after it has dried, bringing up the colours by rubbing on beeswax in turps. – which I am trying, whilst part of the oil dries.' This gouache turned out to be the fore-runner of the oil painting *Shop window with Fern*, and Tom had sent the 'experiment' to me for comment and to keep as a small gift. Unfortunately, I did not like it, and he says in a following April Fool's Day letter 'I'm glad you said straight out that you didn't like the painting – I didn't much myself! It's so nice to have a bit of real criticism instead of a 'mutual back-slapping' business which is what St. Ives is so like.'

Again on June 4th, he writes, 'Then yesterday was the whole of the St. Matthew Passion, which I think is one of the three greatest works ever written (the other two being the B mi Mass and the Ninth Symphony). So I'm afraid Verdi doesn't get much of a showing there! . . . although he is one of my three *favourites* (that being very different from the greatest). But the glorious chorales which keep coming into the Passion ("Oh Sacred Head once wounded") are set to music of all time. Incidentally, the Passion set me painting again . . . .'

By December, 1951 he is able to say as he works on one of his big St. Paul's oils, 'Life is just the picture at the moment; I think about it waking, and dream about it sleeping.'

A letter which he wrote on April 19th, 1951 reveals so much about Tom and how he was affected by all aspects of art and nature. He quotes here from an article in the magazine *Opera*, and follows it with his own most touching comment: "'Janacek is like Bartok, a collector of folk-tunes, he listens to the voices of nature which he delineates in his own musical shorthand – the call of birds when they are sad or in love, the intonation of the voices when he is in conversation with a friend, the voices of quarrelling market-women, the barking of his beloved dogs". I think a composer who can write about the call of birds when they are sad or in love must be a real composer, don't you?'

When I first entered Tom's studio high up in the Carbis Bay house in 1951, I was instantly caught up by the vibrancy of the life-force which sprang out from the assorted canvasses. The colours, the fascinating shapes, and the intensity of feeling were compelling. Down the years I have grown to love and appreciate his paintings more and more, and have always counted it a great blessing indeed to be able to keep so many of them around me.

*Pick-me-ups in St. Ives and the years
before and after*

I first met Tom at the Mansard Gallery in Heals of London when he and Denis Mitchell came up at the end of 1950 to arrange an exhibition of 15 Cornish Artists. I was working there as a junior gallery assistant. The show opened in January 1951, and marvellous names – as contained in the beautiful catalogue by Guido Morris – hung the walls: Barbara Hepworth with her study of surgeons' hands, Ben Nicholson, Alfred Wallis, Patrick Heron and Bryan Wynter among them. If only one could have afforded just one of the works. In those days a salary of £3.50 a week did not allow for such indulgences, and somehow paying on the 'never-never', as we used to call deferred payments in those days – although almost certainly acceptable to the artists – was not even contemplated. Or perhaps I was just too nervous to suggest it. It was at

19

this show that delightful Aunt Alice Early, not specially known for such directness, unexpectedly commented on one of the sculptures 'well, at least all the holes are in the right places!' This instantly elevated his relative to a stature she could hardly have envisaged.

Tom's discovery that an opera magazine lying in the gallery belonged to me began the relationship. I was not then to know the extent of his devotion to music, and this 'find' immediately prompted an invitation to Covent Garden. From that moment we never really looked back. In March he wrote, 'I'm really a terrible person, you know . . . one of my faults (or virtues!) is I like *smells* – any old smells, drains, dead cats but particularly turps. and oil paints. I don't know why I keep telling you all these things – I think it's because I believe you should know the worst before it's too late!' And then, with reference to cementing our relationship he added '. . . I'm afraid it may be a harum-scarum sort of existence at first. I hope you don't mind too much? I always think a millionaire's life must be terribly dull – no washing up or cooking (should be the other way round!), no socks to mend etc.'

I should perhaps add here – lest there be any misunderstanding about dead cats – that Tom had an even *greater* liking for *live* ones, and, beginning with a sad little stray, a steady stream of assorted and much loved felines accompanied us all down the years.

Before long I was invited down to Cornwall, and there I met his mother. I remember how he went to infinite pains to 'smooth the way' for me, and his special emphasis on Mrs. Early's essential kindness I was later to discover was not overstated. But the initial meeting was with a lady of almost forbidding severity, and, in all the circumstances, this may well have been emphasised by her apprehension of me!

Tom had recently emerged from a failed first marriage, he was suffering from totally unpredictable grand-mal epilepsy, and he was out of a 'proper' job. So it must have been extraordinarily difficult for her to receive and welcome a 21-year old unknown quantity. But she did, albeit in a very restrained and unemotional way, and down the many years that followed I grew to admire and love her for herself.

She was the eldest of the seven children of a Methodist minister with Cornish blood in her veins, and from early childhood had cast herself in the role of overseer and example to the younger ones. At the age of 15 she had signed The Pledge, and thereafter would never knowingly touch a drop of alcohol. Two of her three sons, Tom and his youngest brother Jim, occasionally tried to persuade her to take a 'nip', but she would have none of it – indignantly declaring that it tasted like ink. We often wondered how much ink she had drunk. In the early autumn of 1951 I had clearly attempted to lay-down-the-law about possible ways of saving money, and in a very swift reply Tom had incisively stated 'If your little sermon about economising means no more wine, then I'm off! So you can take your choice!'

When, at the wedding of Denis and Jane Mitchell's eldest daughter, Mrs Early's orange juice was – innocently or otherwise – laced with champagne, she enjoyed it so much that for months afterwards she tried – unsuccessfully! – to discover which brand it was because it was the best she had ever tasted. Her magnaminity and dislike of waste outweighed her disgust at once finding a crate of beer left on her doorstep by the Metal Box Company, in which she had some shares, and her swift and uncompromising reaction meant that Denis became the instant recipient of that bit of largesse.

Tom's father was a medical doctor with the Methodist Missionary Society in South China between 1913 and 1936, and Tom, the eldest son, was born in Fatshan, Canton, in December 1914. Two brothers followed in 1918 and 1921. Tom had been baptised Edward Cyril, but there is a story that his father, on looking one day into his pram, exclaimed 'but here is a *real* TOM', and so he got his name. The family was Liberal and Methodist, and through Thomas Early in 1669 the family blanket weaving business was started in Witney, Oxfordshire. In the eighteenth century a number of the family were Quakers, and the non-conformist tradition continued when a thriving Wesleyan Society in Witney included many Earlys. During the nineteenth century, marriage links with a family of silk-weavers introduced Huguenot stock. The spirit of Liberalism prevailed in the Early Blanket Mill, and a true altruism and keen sense of duty towards others was uppermost in the family's dealings. This, allied to the strong Cornish Methodist tradition on his mother's side, was the inheritance.

Many years later my sister-in-law, Anne Early, and I wondered how any of the boys ever came to be conceived, and it was a considerable eye-opener (naturally tinged with due contribution) to discover that, in fact, the circumstances of our parents-in-laws' marriage had really been rather romantic. Dr. Early had been scheduled to go out to China for his first 4-year term as a single man, but the Methodist Missionary Society was forced to reconsider when he refused to go unless he could take his bride. The fact that it made good sense for them to learn the difficult language together in no way detracts from this story.

It also emerged that one of Tom's specific pleasures in marrying me was that the inordinate number of 'black sheep' he discovered in what little family history I had would, at last, put a proper balance on his own – which barely boasted even one!

As was the norm, when Tom reached the age of seven, he was sent back to school in England. He went as a boarder at The Downs near Malvern, which was a Quaker Preparatory School known to the Early family, and in the charge of a 'formidable Head who was, nonetheless, the kindest of men with a fine sense of humour and certainly a great Headmaster'. Music was – and still is – a strong point at the school with professional recitals and gramophone sessions in the headmaster's study. Tom's love for music and singing was fostered in those days. The school had a good library, and reading was encouraged from a very early age. One indignity, however, that ever remained in his memory was being sent back by train to school 'in charge of the Guard'.

Tom had suffered an undiagnosed illness in China when he was about five or six, and he arrived in England looking pale and wan. His relatives were somewhat shocked by his appearance, but his immensely kind Witney grandmother, with whom he stayed in the holidays, speedily set about remedying this. Many years afterwards both his mother and I wondered whether this curious illness, which had left him with months of lethargy, could have remained dormant in his system and been responsible for his later epilepsy.

A cousin with whom Tom and his brothers annually met up, remembers those days as 'a very happy time in a very privileged environment, and where one just took everything for granted'. The days were filled with tennis parties, games of croquet, country walks, and a marvellous game on bicycles in the large Witney garden when it was imaginatively divided up into the various stations of the Great Western Railway. Swimming in the river Windrush behind the weaving sheds of the Early Blanket Mill was another favourite pastime, and occasional concerts in which Tom had a major creative hand were arranged for the benefit of the various 'indulgent' relations and house staff.

In 1929 Tom's mother finally returned home from China, taking a house in Paignton, and in the late 1920s there were glorious summer seaside holidays in Devon and Cornwall 'when Tom was very much the leader of the three brothers, and full of ideas on how to amuse themselves'. This exuberant abundance of ideas was to last throughout his life, and quite certainly impinged on his highly developed and imaginative artist's eye.

In 1928 he entered Greshams, a public school at Holt in Norfolk, and there a very enlightened form of education was practised 'in which any form of corporal punishment was ruled out'. Benjamin Britten was an 'overlapping' pupil, and Tom was more than a little jealous to discover that the future composer was excused certain games in order to devote more time to music. As a consequence, he went so far as to get two front teeth knocked out in a rugby game in the unlikely hope he might be let off, too. He later felt this to have been an almost classically contrived psychological accident. It was here that he developed a keen and lasting delight in the operas of Gilbert and Sullivan, and produced with his brother, Peter, two volumes of libretti under the pseudonyms Seymour and Schwenk!

In 1933 Tom went up to Queen's College, Cambridge, to begin his medical studies, and there, true to his sense of how life in all its available aspects should be spent, made the widest possible use of his time. Whether Tom was 'subtly pressurized' into medicine as the eldest son of a doctor father, and with every material advantage, is debatable. At any rate, he found it not always easy to pass the exams, and he managed to emerge at the end of his three years without a degree. He was still persisting – unsuccessfully – with the Cambridge M.B. Finals up to late 1942. His brother, Peter, later felt that, in any case, 'he had an instinctive preference for "medicine of the mind" rather than for the more physical aspects of the profession.'

It was about this time that Tom underwent a 'vocational assessment' test, and was subsequently advised that a job in the literary world – such as librarianship – could be more suited to his needs. However, he persisted in medicine, and went on to University College Hospital in 1936. It was during this period in the mid 1930s that the first sign of his epilepsy manifested itself. He continued, however, to pursue with all enthusiasm his 'extra-mural' artistic interests in the midst of his medical studies, and finally qualified in 1940. He held initial house-posts at Wembley and Guildford, and a stint at the Seamen's Hospital in Greenwich he particularly remembered for the wonderful painted dining-room there.

In 1941, all three brothers were in London and met up for an after-noon's concert at the Queen's Hall which that night was destroyed during an air-raid. Tom never ceased to mourn its loss, and most especially for its near-perfect acoustics. Years later, in a letter written on Good Friday 1951 he says 'It will be most exciting to see what the Festival Hall is like – if the acoustics are as good as you say, I shall have to stop scratching my hair!'

He never lost an opportunity to register – where appropriate – his feelings and, many years later, following a particularly fine B.B.C. concert in a beautiful old church at Lavenham at which Sir Adrian Boult had conducted, he spotted the great man enjoying a quiet dinner with his wife at a nearby table to our own. Without a moment's hesitation he went over to offer his congratulations, and such was Sir Adrian's courtesy that even with such an interruption he most generously acknowledged this obviously genuine music lover.

In October, 1951 Tom writes '. . . I must say that I have just been listening with tears in my eyes, to a talk on Constant Lambert by Willy Walton in 'Music Magazine'. The fact that he so obviously wasn't used to broadcasting, saying the wrong words and almost stuttering at times, made it all the more moving. Incidentally, his greatest work (perhaps), "Summer's last Will and Testament" is a good example of his fondness for jokes, puns etc., for the poem which is set is about a Will Summers.'

Again later he writes 'I have just been listening to a very interesting talk on a visit to Sibelius in 1929 – by Basil Cameron. They discussed the 4th Symphony, and Sib. made this charming remark: "It's such a relief to me when two men like the same piece of music. It's very different, of course, when it's a woman".'

Later, in 1943, Tom went to take up a post at the E.M.S. Hospital at Shotley Bridge, County Durham, and about that time met his first wife. Thereafter he lived and worked in the north, entering for the first time into psychiatric medicine, until the accident that brought him down to Cornwall.

During my first visit to Carbis Bay and St. Ives in mid-summer, 1951 I met and came to know some of the artists, and began to taste the flavour of that unique place on the Cornish coast. With his customary zest Tom took me around his various haunts, the old tin-mine ruins, stark little chapels, the china clay dumps at St. Austell, and the amazing Minnack Theatre stuck high up on the cliff edge above Porthcurno. The walks we took then and on so many subsequent occasions were unforgettable, with the sometimes almost unbelievable turquoise . . . green . . . blue-into-midnight-blue colour of the sea against the immense drama of the cliffs and fabulous beaches; and the swimming and the picnics with home-made Cornish pasties and delicious 'thunder and lightning' scones all came together to heighten consciousness and make everything hang in a kind of eternity. We were, of course, young and in love.

Tom and Denis Mitchell shared a particular love of churches, and much later on when Denis and Jane were staying with us in Derby, I remember the visit we made to Kelham, then one of the main Anglican religious orders in the country, and how the two men both revelled in the fantastic rounded interior of the chapel. This was the kind of intense experience they shared so many times in their painting and sketching trips around Cornwall.

Whenever funds permitted, Tom got up to London – with a specially well planned trip for the Festival of Britain – and then we would indulge in an orgy of exhibitions and musical events, or just relish a meal – always accompanied by a decent bottle of wine – at his favourite little restaurant, Bertorelli's in Charlotte Street, or the 'Polish Corridor' in Tottenham Court Road. In those days this last was a plush other-worldly speciality tea and coffee house, and it was typical of him that he should have loved this place with its surprisingly strong European flavour. In the midst of all this we did not neglect for one moment to find plenty of time to also indulge – in the most time-honoured way of all – our blossoming relationship.

An interesting comment he makes when writing later in that Festival year of 1951 reads 'I have just been looking again at the "Disasters of War" by Goya (one of the half dozen greatest painters, do you think?) and astonished to find that no. 60 ("No-one could help them") has a face which looks remarkably like that horrifying face of the present day artist, Bacon, in his back view of the man going through a curtain! I suppose I ought to have seen the connection between Goya and Bacon before, but I haven't!'

Among those contemporary artists Tom specially regarded was Paul Klee, and I think he had a not inconsiderable sense of identity with him. Kokoschka had shown an interest in his work at one stage, and Tom had written to him in 1965 with a view to a meeting. What prevented this from taking place is now unclear.

Almost from the beginning of our relationship Tom was trying to get back into medicine – there seemed no earthly hope then of living off painting – and from the beginning he had to contend with a steady stream of polite but negative reactions. The difficulties associated with the nature of his illness, combined with a six-year absence from medical practice, made for a huge problem indeed. He tried for a wide variety of jobs including some as far afield as the Sudan, one with the National Book League, and one as a translator of medical material with a firm based in Switzerland (the location being the main attraction), but all drew blanks. He even considered approaching Sadlers Wells with a view to doing scene painting or designing. In November, 1951 he wrote '. . . going back into medicine (if I ever get a job!) doesn't mean giving up painting . . .' Although in the main he preserved an amazingly buoyant and philosophical attitude, eventually both our spirits began to be seriously undermined. Early in 1952 we broke off our engagement, although in my case this was agreed to with a feeling of near despair. Suddenly life seemed very black and meaningless.

Tom had asked me to marry him within the first week of our meeting (could this have revealed the impetuous element in his temperament?), and finally, in the wake of all the frustrations and disappointments, told me it was too unfair to expect me to make a life with an 'old crock' like him. In some inexplicable and unexpected way, however, the 'break' seemed to almost instantly re-cement our commitment, and with it came an almost uncanny sense of destiny.

It was now mid-1952, and, as if the gods finally took pity on us, Tom was offered a 3-months' job as ship's doctor on a Blue Funnel Line boat going out to Japan. As it happened this also provided the opportunity for another kind of fulfilment before settling down, as Tom had a great love and fascination for Japan and the Japanese people. The group of poems which came directly out of this experience can be seen later in the book.

We married in December 1952 at Wandsworth Registry Office on the first day of one of the last great London 'smogs'. Tom, who was almost 'blindly' walking across Clapham Common with his mother and an aunt, spotted a newsagent looming up out of the gloom, and, with almost fervent glee, rushed in to buy that day's copy of the *News Chronicle*. This, only because it contained his favourite cartoon strip, Colonel Pewter, and without question this constituted quite as great a triumph for him as any other part of that day's celebrations! Totally bemused at the time, his two female relatives never forgot the incident.

Tom had a great sense of the ridiculous, the somewhat lewd and the bawdy, and his appreciation of varying kinds of graffiti – very well stated across the landscape even then – once prompted him to say that, while such often wonderfully witty public indulgences pertained, he had *every* hope for mankind. Walking down the Charing Cross Road with him in those early days was something of an experience, because at every 'suspect' bookstall he would stop, and very audibly roar his appreciation. He was particularly fond of the 'naughty' seaside postcard as personified by Donald McGill, and on one never-to-be-forgotten occasion during a rather 'posh' restaurant lunch a new supply he had stuffed into a totally inadequate pocket suddenly burst out over at least a square yard of floor, treating our nearest neighbours to some quite unexpected 'McGillian' close-ups.

Tom's fondness for a particular brand of humour included Thurber, Ronald Searle and, of course, Edward Lear. Lear, too, had suffered from the 'falling sickness'. This long preserved newspaper cartoon gives a flavour.

"That's Beethoven's fifth."

26

After a brief honeymoon in Cambridge, we returned to London. Tom had managed to get a few weeks locum at a small hospital on the Mile End Road, but getting back into medicine was never going to be easy. No doubt because of this and a mounting inner conflict over the now irrevocable step we had taken we suddenly had our first major ROW. This was quite certainly triggered by some ill-advised provocation from me, but the vehemence of his reaction took me totally by surprise, and, in retrospect, it was perhaps not unlike a 'conscious' fit. He must have been in some *very* severe emotional turmoil to have lost so much control, and only once again in our fifteen years of marriage was such an episode repeated. As Sven Berlin has said, he was essentially an immensely kind and gentle man; but the epilepsy persisted.

Following the end of the London locum, Tom went north for a longer-term locum in a big mental hospital three miles south of Sunderland. Allied to his Cornish background and response to that Celtic land was a strong pull towards things northern, and he had a special affinity with 'Geordie-land'. If he could have found a Geordie in his genes and spoken with a good north country accent he would have been a truly happy man. When in the north-east he delighted in the flattened vowel so that New*car*stle swiftly became New*ca*stle and Sunderland S*oo*nderl*u*nd. He identified keenly with the deprivations of the local people, as he did with the Welsh miners and the tin miners of Cornwall. His feeling for the harsh lives of these last was *very* real. He sometimes spoke of the appalling life-styles of the old Cornish miners, of the endless dreary hours' walk there and back many had just to get to work each day. Deeply conscious of his own comparatively privileged back-ground he felt, I believe, real sorrow that their days were doomed to be all work and *no* play.

His concern had been fostered by experiences during the mid to late 1930s when, during the long college vacations, he had taken part in at least one Quaker work camp digging with the unemployed in Austria. In 1939 he went with his brother Peter to the Rhondda Valley where they stayed with a mining family. There they enjoyed wonderful hospitality for a very small sum, and at the same time were very much exposed to the grim realities of those dark days. These camps were developed in the 1930s both in the U.K. and abroad for schools and colleges to send groups to live for a time with unemployed families, and to help the sick, aged and disabled. All the work was voluntary.

Tom's spirited political interests – in the widest sense – also led to his attending a League of Nations summer course in Geneva in 1935. Throughout most of his adult life his bias was towards Socialism, but his sorrow over the premature death of Gaitskell and his replacement by Wilson in the early 1960s brought some disillusionment in the last years of his life. I vividly remember an election campaign in Derby when Tom spotted our M.P., George Brown (later Lord George-Brown), standing outside the local polling station sporting a vast red rosette in his button-hole. Without losing a moment he rushed over and shook him vigorously by the hand. I was utterly outraged because at that time I intensely disliked George Brown's public image, and only later discovered – when he made an official visit to the hospital – that he was, in fact, compassionate and warm-hearted, and a very good constituency M.P.

For the next eighteen months we lived between the hospital near Sunderland and another large mental institution ten miles out of Durham. Tom's energies were now devoted to cementing his return to psychiatric medicine. A revolutionary new drug, Largactil, had only just been introduced into the treatment of many violent patients, and so there were still the overhang of the old and much less attractive treatments. It was often gruelling. To paint seemed impossible.

It was during this time that my brother died at a very young age, and in totally unexpected and tragic circumstances. We had been married only nine months and Tom had had little chance to really get to know him. I clearly remember his grief when it transpired that an opportunity (through family friends in Cornwall) that might have made all the difference to my brother's state of mind had come just one month too late. Tom's identification with others' needs was profound, and he was everlastingly tinged by the sadness of that particular irony.

Prof. Lionel Haward, a colleague and close friend from those days, remembers:

> First impressions of a person always colour later assessments: they are never entirely eradicated. For this reason, some account of my initial view of Tom deserves mention. It occurred in the Durham County Asylum, then euphemistically renamed Winterton Hospital, and at the time of the patients' annual dance. Strict segregation of the sexes was then in force, and the only time the male patients came to know that Eve and her descendants had appeared as a divine afterthought was on this one annual occasion. In the large hall some five hundred patients of each sex were herded against opposite walls: the ladies looked at their potential partners with all the delicious horror of a spinster finding the neighbourhood rapist under her bed, and the men were held back by a large posse of rugby-size male nurses. As each dance was announced by the bandleader, performing from the safety of the stage, the male nurses would release their grip, and a tidal wave of long-thwarted masculinity

would surge across the floor engulfing the women and dragging them willy-nilly into a maelstrom of movement which was less a waltz or valeta than a cross between whirling dervishes and an Indian rain dance.

It was into this mêlée that Tom suddenly appeared. He was preceded by a line of porters carrying divers boxes containing his worldly goods and chattels, and immediately in front of him was his wife, Eunice, bearing aloft a large standard lamp, like Sister Susannah (who carried the banner). Tom himself carried some large obscure piece of furniture on his head, and the whole safari looked like a scene from Sanders of the River. 'Make way! Make way!' a stentorian voice bellowed, and the milling throng parted like the Red Sea at the approach of the Israelites. The medical staff, arranged in armchairs along the front of the stage like judges at a skating contest, watched in goggle-eyed amazement at the spectacle, and the band continued to render its military two-step. The porters, no longer having to carve their way through a wall of human flesh, fell into step, so that the procession now resembled the March of the Boyards, and, wending its way across the hall, disappeared through a side door, Tom with the big cheerful grin we came to know so well giving a final wave of thanks.

This cheerful Cheshire Cat grin was always heart-warming, and brightened the dullest day. Life in mental hospitals in the early post-war years was fairly gruesome: physical restraint was still in use, electric shock therapy was at its crudest, and the operating theatre always had steam up to rob a continuous stream of patients of complete brain function. The great pharmaceutical revolution of psychiatry had yet to come. Into the milieu of despondency and frustrating inadequacy Tom brought a special quality. He really *cared*. There were doctors probably more efficient than him; there were some possibly more effective; but there were none who were so much in tune with these lost souls that they could reach out, as Tom did, and make them feel cared for, even wanted. He was the archetypal Good Samaritan, giving with love the best of his therapeutic skills. Much more than that, he made them feel human again, no longer society's rejects, and in the warmth of the sympathy, understanding and compassion he offered them, the patients regained some of the dignity of which they had been long deprived.

I had the impression that Tom was not finding it easy to

express himself in his art at this time: the vibes seemed all wrong. But he did have one satisfying outlet for his artistic yearnings. As a long-standing Savoyard he loved Gilbert and Sullivan operas, and one of my more lasting memories is of Tom, in a ward of long-term patients, clutching a wilting daffodil taken from a windowsill vase, parading round the ward and singing 'Twenty lovesick maidens we' from the performance of *Patience* which we had seen the previous week. The obvious delight of the five score inmates, enjoying not only Tom's rendering of the song but marvelling in the fact that here was a doctor who was actually entertaining them and enjoying doing so. Just as the Lakeland poet who, in pensive mood, would recall the sight of daffodils and find his heart with pleasure filled, so I myself, in times of depression during the passing years, have conjured up this vision of Tom and his daffodil. It was more than just a vignette of his natural joie de vivre which shone like a lamp to illuminate even his darkest hours; it was an expression of his deep affinity for, and love of, his fellow men. If Abou Ben Adhem's name led all the rest, Tom's would have been a close runner-up.

The two years in the north and the following three in Wells, Somerset, where Tom took a post as a Junior Registrar were creatively very unproductive, and indeed, by the time we left Wells for Derby in early 1958, he could only say with rather more than faint damning praise of his experience there 'where every prospect pleaseth, and only Man is vile!'

He had, as a great salve to his soul, been able to indulge his passion for music and literature by linking up with a few like-minded people, some of whom became good and lasting friends, and many rewarding hours were spent in a music society near Glastonbury. Some particular friends with whom Tom shared a great love of poetry – he had been deeply affected by Dylan Thomas's death in 1953 – remember him as being 'a great enhancer of life', and these occasions provided the vital refreshment and antidote to the often disturbing realities of life in a 1950s mental hospital.

A great 'highlight' was an excursion with a friend to Covent Garden to see an acclaimed production of Berlioz' *The Trojans*, and such an event would lift his naturally buoyant spirit quite astonishingly higher. On a similar rather high-flown operatic occasion, Tom had had to stand up against his seat to allow a late and voluminously dressed lady to pass. Somehow his trouser zip got caught up in the dress, and the result was a spectacular crab-walk-in-close-embrace back down the central aisle to the manager's office where the now almost hysterical owner of the gown was finally released. Not once did Tom indicate – although nearly convulsed with suppressed laughter – that this was anything other then part of the interesting pattern of everyday experience. He returned to his seat entirely prepared to participate fully in the ensuing artistic feast and, of course, he did!

A small insight into how he was able to handle such a situation is revealed in a letter written in April, 1951. 'Puzzle for you. One day this week I was listening to the morning Elgar records, and they were playing that glorious bit from the slow movement of the 2nd. symphony – and again I could have wept for joy! An hour later I was listening eagerly to the absurd gossip of the Dales, and lapping it all up . . . how is one so quickly able to change from the heights to the depths (if they are); and do you? I am quite certain I could listen to Gerontius bang next to Take it from Here, and not get a wit the less out of glorious Gerontius. Probably I'm at bottom (where one does most of one's listening) frivolous. Well, well.'

A colleague and friend from Wells also remembers that 'when I first met Tom in 1955 he was working in a psychiatric hospital but not then actively painting. Whenever I visited his home, however, I was very aware of his pictures. I was impressed by the wide range of his work, his use of strong colours – although strong the colours were in harmony. He showed an interest in, even a fascination for, objects others would not have noticed. But there were few people in his pictures. Yet the overwhelming impression Tom made as a person and a doctor was of someone with an extremely gentle and sensitive understanding of others, relating to each one as a valued individual. I never remember him showing aggression towards another person, although his great sense of humour and fun enabled him to express anger without being destructive.'

Professor Haward recollects:

In Somerset, Tom reflected the antipathetic vibrations of the professional community in which he found himself, but staying with him in his own home brought fresh insights into the character and personality of this gentle man. Here, too, we were able to see for the first time the (then) full range of his paintings, some of which made an unusually strong impact, and possessed a haunting quality which engendered emotional overtones when the image of them was recalled.

One in particular, his view of London's South Bank, which was familiar to me from many childhood 'sorties' over Hungerford Bridge, captured my attention and aroused emotions in a way and for reasons not easy to analyze. I took a

31

photograph of this painting, and in later years spent a considerable amount of time wondering what particular aspect of my psyche it touched so deeply. There were other paintings by Tom which had a not dissimilar effect, as if, in exploring his own inner being and clothing it in the facade of reality, he had somehow touched some similar and long-repressed experience from my own past.

Many years previously, I had collected and studied many paintings by TB patients in a sanatorium, and come to learn how the personal problems created by their condition found symbolic outlet in the colours, forms, and subjects of their art. While Tom was not a TB patient, nonetheless he had his own medical problems, and this gave his paintings their own special quality of personal depth which could trigger off associations deep in the unconscious of the observer, at least in those who coincidentally tuned into the same wavelength.

Tom was a rich source of stimulation to everyone about him, and leaving him at the end of my holiday was to experience sensory deprivation.

Even in the worst moments his sense of fun never completely deserted him, and, at one of the annual New Year Patients and Staff Fancy Dress Balls, he allowed himself to be disguised as a 1920s debutante. Complete with wig, bow lips and long ropes of beads draped over an exaggeratedly inflated bodice he was totally unrecognisable. During the ensuing dancing he subsequently learned more about his own sex than he had probably acquired at any other stage of his career!

His popularity with certain patients was also legion as he actually prescribed for them a daily 'dose' of Scrumpy. I have also been reminded that he was remembered at the hospital as a 'true gentleman'. But it was here in Wells that he suffered the accident which was eventually to lead to his death. Returning home from a night-duty call he fell into an unguarded hole in the grounds, and broke his leg. Ironically, as has already been said, it had nothing to do with his epilepsy.

Denis and Jane Mitchell spent a couple of holidays with us during this period at Wells between 1955 and 1958, and Denis never failed to urge Tom to 'keep on with his painting'. But somehow the emotional climate there was still anathema to him, and he just could not get going creatively. No doubt the coming to terms with that hard decision to return to medicine and working through those early years of remarriage played a key role in this. Once in desperation he took the car and drove it into Wells and back, and this surely indicated – with all the implications of

Rusty boiler,
Pendeen Head.
Watercolour 1946.

St Ives. Oil on paper 1946.

Son et Lumière.
Oil 1964.

This Lunar Landscape.
Oil 1965.

Cape Cornwall. Oil 1950.

Ships at Lelant.
Oil 1950.

Boat with crane.
Oil c. 1948.

*Skeleton of half
built ship.*
Oil c. 1947/8.

Truro.
Watercolour 1949.

Fields below Trencrom. Oil 1946/7.

Minehouse. Oil 1948.

Shop Window with Fern. Oil 1951.

Still Life and Studio Windows. Oil c. 1948.

St Paul's, London. Oil 1962/3.

St Ives Bay in Snow. Oil c. 1947/8.

St Michael's Blackfriars. Watercolour 1950.

South Bank and Shot Tower. Watercolour 1948.

such an action – something of the awful frustrations and pressures he was suffering at that time. It was not until our move to the Midlands in early 1958 that the urge to express himself in paint began to resurface.

Throughout the 1950s and early 1960s we went down to Cornwall, and St. Ives and Carbis Bay in particular, every year. The final stage of the rail trip was the local St. Erth to St. Ives line, and, once on this from the mainline, the full flooding sensation of the Celtic country overtook us. For the next two or three weeks, life was to take on another dimension, full of encounters with friends in the artists' community.

At the Castle Inn, then run by Denis's brother Endell Mitchell, we would meet up with whoever happened to drop in that day – maybe Terry Frost, Sven Berlin or Peter Lanyon amongst others, and certainly Denis himself was never too far away. There was always a tension in the air and a sense of camaraderie, even if some of the talk was full of heat or indignation, and it felt good to be alive. The atmosphere was charged, despite the fact – or perhaps because of it – that much of life then was for many of the artists anything but safe and sure. For Tom, even such limited access to this degree of vitality was a great restorative.

Always there were the studios to visit, but our attempts to see John Wells at Newlyn did not always meet with instant success. If he happened not to be feeling in the mood he would stick his head out of an upstairs window, say something audibly inhospitable, and withdraw it immediately! The front door would then remain firmly shut, and it was obvious there was no point in staying. Johnny is a true eccentric, and you took him as you found him. Like Tom, he had been a doctor, and finally quitted his practice on The Scillies to give all his time to painting.

On one ever memorable occasion – which Denis never allowed us to forget! – Tom and I were visiting the St. Ives Gallery summer exhibition, and we were strongly drawn to a painting marked up as being by John Wells for £25. It did, however, bear all the hallmarks of a Ben Nicholson, and we both came to the conclusion that Johnny must have been coming under Nicholson's influence. So taken were we with it and feeling we could just about afford the asking price, we informed the gallery assistant, who rejoiced in the name of Miss B. Good and who, on discovering that we knew Johnny, rushed to the 'phone to advise him. He, in turn, rushed over to the gallery, but on seeing the painting his face turned an almost instant puce, and, with a roar of rage, he pronounced the picture NOT TO BE HIS and that we must *all* be some particular brand of idiot. On this note and without stopping for more he then stormed out! Of course the work *was* a Ben Nicholson, it had been mistakenly labelled, and the real price suddenly trebled! It went instantly out of our reach, and, horribly conscious of the awful faux-pas, we actually settled for a genuine John Wells instead. We never regretted it.

Peter Lanyon and his wife Sheila we visited most years, and their house, Little Parc Owles, seemed always full of their ever increasing family. Peter was unfailingly willing to show us his latest work, and – most vividly – I remember him taking us up through his large garden to the converted double garage which served as his studio, and which seemed to be filled with a great number of amazing paintings inspired directly from his gliding experiences. Peter was a very personable and volatile character, full of life and with very definite ideas. Whether for or against a cause or situation, he certainly never minced words if he was at war with an issue! I think he took his art *very* seriously because, when he was made a Bard for his services to painting in Cornwall, I inadvertently laughed at the notion of him dressed in his long ceremonial 'nightgown'. He was not amused. It was a tremendous shock to hear of his tragically premature death as a result of a gliding accident in 1964.

Sheila Lanyon, in remembering Tom, says he was 'a lovely man and one of the TRUE ones'. She had had to learn very quickly to sort out the TRUE from the FALSE in the highly charged world of art.

Her story of Tom's Tuckingmill Chapel picture – now regrettably lost from her collection – apparently caused endless merriment down the years. In the bottom right hand corner of the painting under the shadow of the great Weslyan Chapel he had put in the little Tuckingmill Hotel with only the TUCK part of the name visible. Peter, who originally owned it, had instantly – but not literally – converted the T into an F.

We always enjoyed browsing in Robin and Dicon Nance's cabinet-making workshop down on the Wharf in St. Ives, and the brothers' craftsmanship was impressive. They were so much a part of that creative community, linking in sympathetically with the other arts, and showing works by the various local artists in amongst their own fine pieces. As a one-time member of the Heals' scene I immensely appreciated this approach, and it was always good to exchange news and views with them.

Invariably we went into George Downing's rather dark and set-far-back bookshop where somehow the owner seemed curiously to resemble his premises. A big, quiet, kindly man, George most generously gave regular space for the artists to show their work, and Tom had been among the exhibitors there. Later George went abroad, and was tragically killed.

To enter Bernard Leach's Pottery was inevitably an 'experience', and to see there the Master and his work. I was familiar with the Leach ware – again through Heals – where his pots were displayed in the Craftsman's Market adjacent to the Mansard Gallery, but it was altogether different to visit the St. Ives location, and to occasionally encounter the great man himself.

Willie Barns-Graham has reminded me that at one time Tom helped Bryan Wynter's wife, Susan Lethbridge, paint toys – little horses and carts – in her Digey studio, and that she herself had made a drawing of him at work. This drawing is now privately owned, but can be seen reproduced in the Barns-Graham retrospective catalogue.

I have treasured down the years a handful of the most beautiful catalogues produced for various exhibitions by Guido Morris, and even now find myself in a kind of confused wonderment at his apparent ambition to be a guard on the London Underground. This he realised (although whether truly out of ambition or necessity I cannot be sure), but not before – thank goodness – he had left a wonderful legacy in print on handmade paper.

Tom was Denis Mitchell's first 'painting partner'. Denis and his wife, Jane, became staunch friends, and we especially loved to see them during these annual Cornish visits, and we were invariably welcomed into their modest home high above St. Ives. Jane, with her hair piled high and her beautiful luminous blue eyes reflecting the colour of the sky, might be struggling with a load of washing from the line in the yard, but we would always be given a cup of tea or coffee, and invited to a meal later. The hospitality was warm and simple and full of laughter and good 'gossip'. Denis was one of those rare people who made me laugh on sight, and this never diminished through all the years I knew him. He had within him a marvellous inexhaustible well of humour and humanity, and this was, of course, what made him into the man we knew, and to whom so many were drawn. Even in those early days way back at the beginning of the 1950s – and before – he would 'hold court' in his somewhat sombre studio above Fore Street, and we would all gather quite naturally around him. His innate wisdom and paternal qualities were in evidence even then, and somehow everyone must have felt 'safe' with him.

He was certainly not, however, without his problems, and as the provider to a family of four life was, over a long stretch of time, a constant concern. Barbara Hepworth, to whom he was an assistant for many years, paid him not a lot, and once when Tom and I were standing talking to him in the road, he suddenly spotted his bank manager looming into view, and promptly bolted down a side street. He just could *not* face the man in *any* circumstances at that moment. How often it must have been like that. But Denis was a man of vision and tenacity who had, quite certainly, a keen sense of his own destiny, and so would never allow himself to be deflected by the difficulties of the moment. Jane has confessed that sometimes when they were especially hard pressed and not a little desperate, she felt *very* cross that Denis would never consider selling anything. Those precious things they had been given or acquired, like a well-known artist friend's painting or pot, he would *never* part with. Always he had faith that something else would turn up – and it did. A piece of his own sculpture would be sold, and the day would be saved.

During his eleven years with Barbara Hepworth, whenever a V.I.P. or the press visited the studio, Denis would be dismissed from the scene. The fact that he had become such an expert in interpreting her requirements, and was thus very valuable to her, never altered this state of affairs. Nonetheless, with his characteristic sense of balance and fairness he never underestimated the benefits he derived from working with her, and has paid her, indeed, his own tribute. A rather amusing comment made by Tom in a letter dated March 26th, 1951 says, 'Have spent most of the day over in St. Ives, taking photos of paintings – my own, Denis's and Terry  Frost's. Incidentally, I saw a huge long lorry drawn up outside Hep's studio with Denis, Terry, Johnny Wells and 3 other men getting the sculptures in position. No sign of Barbara Hep. Rather funny, I thought, one piece of stone like this: had "MALE" written on it in big letters. It certainly didn't look much like it – perhaps it had been broken off in the shift!'

A visit with Tom to their near neighbour, Miss E.H. Hodgkin's house on Headland Road in Carbis Bay in 1951 brought me into my most vivid experience up to then of Barbara Hepworth's work. The house smelt sickeningly of cats, but this faded almost instantly into nothingness as we entered a main room to see framed against the light on a deep window-ledge her most beautiful serravezza marble, *Group 1 (Concourse)*. A small group of figures so perfectly juxtapositioned, translucently lovely against the light, and so compellingly noble.

Later, in 1954, I went with Tom to the Whitechapel Gallery in London where Barbara was to have a major exhibition, and there we found her coolly and authoritatively attending to the arranging of the sculptures. I was struck then by a sense of her remoteness, and of a personality to which I could not relate. A return to St. Ives after a long absence in recent years and a visit to her memorial studio unexpectedly altered that long-standing attitude, and, as with that sight of *Concourse* and the *Surgeons' Hands* at Heals, I found myself strangely moved by some flash of 'recognition' of the *real* person so welded to her art.

Tom's mother, who became very fond of the Mitchell family, made it possible for Denis and Jane to have occasional holidays, including a couple abroad, and, wherever she could, helped them in practical ways.

Only shortly before he died Denis told me of an incident that took place on one of Mrs Early's visits to his mother, Blanche, who had always lived with them. As Mrs. Early was leaving the house she put into Denis's hand a sealed envelope which she asked him to open only after she had left. In it was a cheque for £100 which, in a quite remarkable way, exactly covered the sum Denis had, without warning, been required to pay back to his bank within a week. Tom's mother could not possibly have known anything of that, and Denis could scarcely believe it. He could never have paid it back at such short notice, and was desperate.

Mrs Blanche Mitchell, too, was a marvellous character in her own right, and we always immensely enjoyed seeing her. She was very good to the family, and had shared their lives almost from the beginning.

It was thrilling when Denis and Jane had a real 'stroke of luck' in managing to purchase a house in Newlyn into which they moved in 1969. It was here, too, that Denis shared with Johnny Wells an old school building ideally converted into their studios, and here so much of his splendid later work was done.

The artists often exchanged works with each other, as they certainly could rarely – if ever – afford to buy, and in this perfect artist's house, with its magnificent views across Mounts Bay, all the 'treasures' of an immensely generous and creative life are to be found.

The years of grace

We moved to Derbyshire early in 1958 when Tom had taken another post as Registrar in the big county mental hospital three miles out of Derby. Although it was by no means to be counted as north of the country, he had settled for this as being the next best thing – and infinitely preferable to Wells.

We lived in a small rented house outside the grounds, where we were cheek-by-jowl with other 'medics' and hospital staff. The medical superintendent, as he was then still called, was a kindly paternalistic character who knew virtually everyone in the place by name. He had a considerable empathy with Tom.

The first two years, however, were neither the easiest nor happiest for either of us, and, following a particularly bad fall when Tom fractured his jaw during a seizure, I finally 'seized up' myself. It was then that a book I had been given by the hospital chaplain came into its own.

This was to do with a place of healing in Kent, and as I then needed help and healing quite as much as – if not very much more than – Tom, I went to investigate. Later Tom, who was always 'open' to new experience

– but in this instance perhaps rather more for my sake – agreed to try it for himself, and there we received much lasting benefit. His epilepsy never was actually 'cured', but a new flowering of his creative energies was released.

In 1958/9 he joined a class at the College of Art in Derby. There he met up with the tutor, Keith Richardson-Jones, Michael Miller, David Ainley, Ian Breakwell, Dennis Hawkins and others, who before long were getting themselves together as a group of artists whose works could be publicly displayed. The meetings, initially held in Keith's house and later in ours in Derby, saw the usual animated discussion and dissension, but finally the first exhibition of the newly-formed Derby Group was held in the Derby Museum and Art Gallery in 1961. The show caused an uproar in the town, and led to a public meeting. Out of all the furore, the artists emerged with – if anything – a reinforced determination to carry on. If nothing else, they had achieved *a response* from the general public.

Over the ensuing years a number of exhibitions were held at The Bear Lane Gallery, Oxford, The Whitworth in Manchester, The University, Nottingham, and at The Hampstead Arts Centre, London and elsewhere. At last, Tom was getting the vital stimulus and the invigorating exchanges with other artists he had so lacked in those middle 1950s years, and – occasionally – he sold a painting.

In 1962, Tom was elected to the Midland Group of Artists in Nottingham, and showed in such mixed exhibitions as Midland 21. In 1965 he had a one-man show at the Midland Group Gallery, which Denis Mitchell came up to open and which, in the event, was to be his last major exhibition.

Always he preserved his own integrity and originality, but now the paintings he was making had another 'feel' about them. Interestingly the big St. Paul's paintings of 1951/2 seem to provide the link between the St. Ives period and the later works, and it is almost as if the 'lean' in-between years merely kept hanging in a kind of suspended time all that was just waiting to come out. The colours were as strong and vibrant as ever, the medium now used almost entirely oils, and, although not the same, the dynamic was surely unchanged.

Once or twice he made a series, as with the Lily Crucifix paintings inspired by the lovely medieval stained glass window in Long Melford church, Suffolk, and a friend from that time says that 'his art, for her, was always highly original and imaginative, with a unique interpretation and use of colour. Even the titles of some pictures were very original, i.e. *Settembrini's Dream* with its lovely use of many different greens, and *Lunar Landscape* which is depicted as though one is looking out of a space capsule.'

Another friend, whilst going through a difficult 'patch', remembers 'having the opportunity of staying alone for a week [in my London flat] during the 1980s surrounded by a number of Tom's paintings, absorbing their life, colour, lines and vision, and gradually feeling healed, integrated and blessed'.

It was more than once suggested to me that Tom was really a religious painter, and, indeed, if the essence of the inner man is expressed through paint, then he was. As he says in a letter of March 17th, 1951 '"Praise to the Holiest in the Height, And in the depth be Praise — etc." always makes me weep with joy. Although not a religious person in the conventional sense, I believe that Art and Religion are so bound up with one another — as you see in old Siena, Florence etc.'

Writing a few weeks later he adds, 'Although I haven't been a church-goer for a long time, I don't think I've ever lost my feeling for God in the trees, bushes, cats and dogs, other people etc., as opposed to the white-bearded Michaelangelo God or the Blake God, both of whom I have always thought to be impressive but utterly impossible, and a bit absurd.'

In a letter to a colleague dated Sunday January 27th, 1963 Tom writes:

Let us take Christianity first. Except for the rare intellectual nearly all of us are a great deal more than we care to admit to being creatures of our childhood learning as well as our much earlier forgotten emotional experiences; before I was 18 I had been influenced by Methodism, the Quakers and the Church of England; by none very deeply, and none of the experiences moved me to anything like the extent that contact with Art, first experienced in my 'teens, or Politics in my 20s. Whereas I have never lost a sense of the all-importance of the Arts and of Politics (in its broadest sense; I perhaps no longer feel the urgency I felt in the mid 1930s, you remember it I expect, confronted with the growing menace in Europe and unemploy-ment at home), Christianity has for me taken a back seat most of the time. Later I discovered that painting pictures, for me, was a pipeline, a source of tapping the oil of the unconscious (I found that in painting the picture took on a life of its own, that maybe one could sit back and admire the finished product, but creation was a battle, as Picasso said).

It seems to me that my interest was in things spiritual only in the sense that 'Veni Creator Spiritus' is – Come, Holy Ghost, our Souls inspire – which can be said about anyone who is moved deeply and creatively about almost any subject. You may also point out that I an not strongly directed towards HOW things happen in the human psyche, so much as concerned in letting them happen to the best of my ability (the Spirit moving over the face of the water); and you would be right. So that anything in the nature of deep psychotherapy would inhibit or actually dry up the hidden well, source of my talent. Whereas the kind of job I am doing now, dull though it seems at times, 'never getting me anywhere' etc., actually has two great advantages (apart from the spare time): 1. am seldom deeply involved in anyone's emotional difficulties, and 2. I derive quite a satisfaction from attending to humble people's humble wants. Nothing that will get me a Bishopric or the P.R.C.P., but I wouldn't know what to do with those exalted posts if I was offered them on a plate!

Down the years many people, on meeting Tom for the first time, almost always believed he must be analysing them. In fact nothing was further from the truth. He was much too interested in the interaction between them and himself to ever consider anything else. He had the great ability to 'switch off' from that side of his life, to just enjoy people as people and to enter wholeheartedly and unreservedly into matters of moment.

In 1961 he allowed himself to be persuaded to come with me into a silent Retreat. I was sure that a whole weekend of restricted speech would be nothing short of bliss for him, but I could not have been more wrong. Less than twenty four hours into the Silence and, in a kind of desperation, he seized the opportunity for a long country walk. Coming unexpectedly upon a cattle auction he paused to rejoice in the sound of voices, inadvertently nodded, and just missed buying himself a cow.

Another incident involving a farm animal was when, as duty doctor, he was urgently asked to see a pig down on the Home Farm. As the result of a fierce fight one had sustained a terrible bite, and was likely to bleed to death. Without any hesitation he went straight down, staunched the bleeding, sewed back the piece of almost severed flesh, and then just got on with his more 'normal' duties. As a colleague observed, 'he never minded what he did'.

In 1963/4 we were able to buy, for the first time, our own house, and we were lucky enough to find a place in Derby – three miles away from the hospital – and built by a builder for himself in 1888. It was a house for an artist with the main rooms overlooking a charming old-fashioned garden, a verandah extending the full width of the property, and a flagpole (minus flag) to boot. Tom, who was not given to such excesses over mere 'pedestrian' bricks and mortar, fell in love with it, and it was good to be distanced from the hospital. There we spent the remaining three and a half years of his life. A friend remembers from her childhood that their Derby house was noted for the amount of 'art' it contained. My memories here are those of a young child and growing teenager. Not only did the walls seem to be covered in various paintings – all originals – but art was everywhere in its various forms. Tom's influence on me through his own work and the impact this house made created within me a growing and permanent love of the 'art world'.

I went to the Derby house but rarely, yet I can still identify the sculpture, the paintings, the music and the beautifully crafted furniture which was there. His paintings ranged from – to my child's eyes – the impossibly enormous to the small and minutely detailed early works of his Cornish days. He integrated his whole self into them, and work also included the calligraphy of a friend such as the piece of the Hippocratic Oath which so lovingly intertwined his love of the creative nature of man with his medical work and beliefs.

As a nurse I can now look in surprise at the openness of spirit he displayed towards others. This led, for instance, to my mother moving from the position of being one of his psychiatric patients to us as a family becoming friends of the Earlys and later staying with them. As we are here talking about the 1950s, I suspect that his attitudes towards his patients were pretty revolutionary. For this he appeared to command much respect, however, as I was to see by the numbers of people who attended his funeral. Tom's funeral was the first I ever attended.

Wholeness was part of his philosophy of life, and he loved beauty in all its forms. Quality of life appeared to be everything. He encouraged this in me, and it was with him and Eunice that I went to my first art exhibitions as a young girl. I distinctly remember the Nottingham exhibition; an exhibition of art and flowers in a church; an exhibition in Derby, and one in the Lincolnshire countryside. He would listen to what I had to say on the subject, and encourage me to be a critic and a judge and enjoy what was in front of me. No-one appeared to him to be too young to appreciate or take part in what was around them.

Another pleasure of the Derby house was that I used to sleep in Tom's studio – on a narrow couch bed under the eaves, with the smell of the paints, his tobacco, and the turps around me. I remember paintings on the easel half-completed, and always felt what a privilege and delight it was to sleep there. (I also used to secretly hope I was the ONLY one allowed to sleep there!)

41

I treasure his memory, and the knowledge of knowing that I once knew a very gifted and creative person. A kindly man with a pipe – a whole man.

In his studio high up in the attic Tom would paint sometimes to the accompaniment of Wagner's entire *Ring Cycle* or to any other piece of music that suited his mood. In August, 1951 he had written 'I won't make your mouth water, but I believe I have heard Meistersinger twice this summer – glorious opera it is, especially for painting to, as it must be easily the longest opera ever written – lasting over 6 hours! I have got on quite a bit with the big oil "butchers shop window" [this was renamed *Shop window with fern*] same as I sent you, only I hope it will turn out better. At the moment it seems to be going in the direction of a Ben Nicholson abstract . . . Whether anything will come of it, Time and Fate alone can tell, though I hope they'll be kind! Before I forget this, doesn't it seem funny to you that I don't much mind about *seeing* an opera – it's almost as good on the wireless, and better when one can paint to its strains! For that matter, I never care if I understand the language – German or Italian – or not; for me the music's the thing. I suppose what comes in at one ear comes out in the brush. Anyhow, I have always felt that most of the plots chosen by opera writers would be better sunk in the sewers of Venice (tho that would be rather hard luck on the Lido!).'

I think it has been truly said that Tom was an artist first and a doctor second. He would never allow a week to begin without scanning the papers for opera, concert and exhibition news, and was always on the alert for the innovative experience. So his love for Lambert, Rubbra, Stravinsky and Berg was as profound as his devotion to Mozart, Handel, Sibelius and Verdi – from these last three he got the 'greatest joy' – and a potentially great rendering in the right setting of *The St. Matthew Passion* or Walton's *Balshazzar's Feast* he would travel miles to hear. One of the last trips we made to London in 1966 was to see the splendidly mounted Masada exhibition, and the interest and excitement this generated in him was extraordinarily infectious. Out of such experiences would sometimes emerge a painting – although there was not necessarily an obvious linkage. As Tom himself has suggested, it is the influences of the various art forms working at a sub-conscious level which flow together to make the finally created piece.

During the early 1960s we occasionally incorporated into our trips to Cornwall visits to Terry and Kathleen Frost. They had, by this time, moved to Banbury in Oxfordshire, and there we were regaled by Terry's colourful personality and vibrant lifestyle and exchanged gossip and views on the art scene at large. Terry has an immense energy and drive, a force which Tom did not by then physically possess, but which was, nonetheless, there deeply contained in his innermost being. When Tom died, Terry accompanied Denis Mitchell in particularly bleak winter weather all the way up to Derby for his funeral.

A three-weeks' trip to France, Germany and Italy in 1963 took us first to painting and sculpting friends in Paris, and then on to Heidelberg to visit a much loved German friend and her lovely old Free Church minister father. Although Tom spoke relatively little German and the pastor no English, the rapport between them was deep and immediate, and a kind of wonderful unspoken language existed between them. It was a true meeting of kindred spirits, and to this day the impact it made on those around them is still remembered.

Professor Lionel Haward again writes:

> Each old mental hospital, created a century or more ago by the Victorian Lunacy Acts, possessed its own particular ethos and milieu, and it seemed to me that each brought out some new or different facet of the artistic complexity I saw in Tom. It was not merely a chameleon-like reflection of the changing nature of his surrounding, but a deepening maturity and a developing weltanschaung born of his experiences and the many influences deriving from his artistic receptivity and expression. In the north he had been Clown Extraordinaire, full of high spirits and a youthful zest for life one could only envy. In the south-west, music, if not his raison d'être, was at least one of the more prominent threads in the tapestry of his life; at the same time he retained that special jocundity which makes poets gay and lesser mortals glad to share his company.
>
> Now in Derby in the early to mid 1960s this was a different Tom to the one I had known earlier. It was a quieter, more thoughtful Tom, one in repose yet suggesting even greater depth than heretofore; a still water, running deep. His Lamp of Destiny shone as brightly, but in more muted colours. His cheerful grin still illuminated the lives of those about him, but in casual moments when caught off-guard, his face had a fathomless look about it, like one who has peered through the Painted Veil, and contemplates the implications of what he has seen. Light and Shade were the fluctuating themes of this visit: just occasionally Tom seemed to enter some invisible penumbra as a sad but not unpleasant shadow passed over his face, making him look like some careworn but contented traveller, waiting patiently to be ferried over the Styx and finish his

43

journey. Then just as suddenly he would emerge into the sunlight of reality and be his old cheerful self again, full of jokes, anecdotes and reminiscences.

I never saw Tom again, and felt immeasurably diminished by his passing. Never have I felt the truth of John Donne's words so acutely. To know Tom was to be touched by a special quality such that one was never the same again. His essence is encapsulated within one's memory, so that in some intangible way he is ever present even if out of our awareness. In that sense he still lives on, influencing unconsciously the lives of all who knew him, moving them imperceptibly towards those ideals Plato saw laid up in heaven, and imbuing them with a moiety of his own singular sense of fun. Moreover, he has left those who knew him a rich legacy of images of himself, both humorous and profound, which in recall brings him back into our ken, lightening our cares with silent laughter or bringing us into serious evaluation of our own contribution to the present state of mankind.

These intangible gifts will, alas, disappear as we, their custodians, follow Tom across the Ferry. But he also left an endowment of something more tangible and permanent, the paintings which form the main concern of this book. Through them, in the years to come, those who never knew him will look at his creations and be touched as they see something of the man behind the canvas and oils. Through the coming years people will be able to enjoy, through his art, a unique view of the world as perceived by Tom; many will find it an interesting or satisfying experience; some, like myself, will be subtly changed by the experience. It is this ability to create, and endow with the power that influences lives as yet unborn, that marks the true artist and the great thinker, and brings man the nearest he can come to immortality.

By early 1967 Tom had begun to display symptoms which were causing concern (unknown to me) among his colleagues, but not yet to me. At that time my distress was caused by his increasing slowness, which left me with a sense of almost unbearable helplessness and frustration. His painting seemed to be suffering, and it was only when we went up to Iona that summer that the full extent of his malaise manifested itself. On walking up a steep incline he found himself distressingly out of breath, and from then onwards these symptoms steadily increased. A brief trip to Bruges in the autumn found him more than once near to collapse, and yet somehow his response to the glories of the city and the Hans Memlings and other Flemish painters remained undiminished and still reflected that eager inner quality of his.

We returned home to seek immediate medical advice, and it was then discovered that he was suffering from an enlargement of the heart. The underlying cause, however, remained maddeningly elusive. Then one morning in very early December he just could not make it to the hospital. He had struggled for months, and could struggle no more.

He was taken into hospital where his condition steadily worsened, and by the third week it was clear he was not responding to any of the treatments. During that time he made just one special and urgent request which was for a record-player and the music of Monteverdi. The kindness of a friend provided one, and the records quickly followed.

Just at that time, too, his youngest brother Jim, who was a vet, and extraordinarily fortuitously on a special assignment to Derbyshire, was able to spend much time with him, and together they shared a fraternal experience of an unexpectedly close kind. An altogether remarkable series of events took place during those last days, and, when the then Archdeacon of Leicester (who was directly linked with the Home of Healing referred to earlier) came by special request to anoint Tom, so affected was he by the whole experience that he asked if he might use it as material to encourage others.

Tom spent those final days in his lone room – how he wanted to be home – infilling himself with the works of that supreme seventeenth century master, and, as a friend later said, dying with immense dignity to the strains of sublime music.

He died at seven o'clock on Christmas morning, just five days away from his 53rd birthday.

Our own hospital chaplain and long-standing friend who came to be with me just after he died writes:

Is anyone weak: I share his weakness
These words don't imply that Dr. Tom was a second St. Paul, but came to me as I pictured Tom Early at the Pastures Hospital, Mickleover.

As chaplain, I can remember standing in the chapel porch as Tom walked by with his hair and his rolled umbrella flapping in the breeze. He plodded towards the Main Building slightly bent but purposeful, dogged if a little fragile.

This fragility helped Tom with his tender loving care alongside the "chronically ill" patients from the first world war, and with the battered and bruised from the subsequent depression and the hospital's "institutional neurosis". The patients sensed the strength in Tom's gentleness and the gentleness in his strength. He was his own person. His humanness confirmed theirs as Essie and Fred, Wilf and Mary.

Maybe, in his art, Tom was combing the open beauty of Cornwall and the closed-in beauty of a psychiatric hospital to find an integration between them? The starkness of locked wards and padded rooms was giving way to a more controlled but, in some ways, a less creative madness. Tom would have preferred to know that the patients were in happy gangs working with the pigs, or in the gardens, rather than sat in a factory-like room packing boxes to make belts, from manufactured bits of metal and strips of rubber, for car seats.

Others, more professional than myself, might see in Tom's canvasses the paradox which I saw in his personableness. His stature was his tolerance and his humanity; his status was simply being Tom with the staff and Dr. Early with the patients.

Perhaps one could say that Tom's heart was in his art, and common humanity, wrought within a profession which was possibly chosen for him but which he might not have chosen. He was able to "sit where they sat" and to rejoice with those who rejoiced and to weep with those who wept. A lovely person.

The male nurses who had been attending him confessed it had been the greatest privilege to nurse him. There had been no words of complaint, and, at the last, he merely said 'how sad he was to leave'. There had been much final suffering, despite all the best efforts of the medical staff, and it only later emerged that he had, in fact, died as a direct consequence of the accident all those years before in Wells. The resulting 'complication' could have been expected to kill him at least a decade sooner, and it was in that moment I realised we had been given a whole ten years' 'grace'.

In July, 1951 Tom had written: 'Peter Warlock. You know, that book is one of the four or five from which I just can't escape (I must have read them a hundred times or more each). But he certainly was a fascinating character; you must hear some of his songs, and what a pity I forgot, I could have played you "The Curlew", a lovely setting of several of Yeats' poems, as we have the records. (There is a very funny bit about his acrimonious letters with Yeats over the setting rights, and how he finally sent Yeats a P.C. of one of the zoo's weird storks, which stand for hours on just one leg. Have you seen them?) But I think the best bit is the dance he performed on Charing X station, when he was living out at Eynsford.

'It's also very tragic at the end, though I am inclined to agree with

Gray that he had come to the end of his talent. As he says, the old age of a Verdi, a Titian, a Goethe, can be very affecting, but there is nothing so futile as an artist repeating himself over and over again, and I suspect the best cure for those suffering from the disease of youthful end-all is probably to give up art altogether. After all, there have been plenty of geniuses like Keats, Shelley etc. who came to their end whilst still young, and I don't see any reason why they should have killed themselves (which is what they did, even though it took the form of consumption with Keats and a boat accident in the gulf of Spezia with Shelley).'

Despite adding 'Please don't take all this too seriously', I now dare to suggest that Tom had been given *just* the right amount of 'extra' time needed to say *all* that he had to say. He had been spared – against all the finally revealed medical 'odds' – for another whole decade, and in those years he had entered into that second flowering of creative activity, the results of which – together with all those early works from his St. Ives years – may now perhaps, at last, be shared with a much wider audience. There is, after all, a time and a place for everything.

EUNICE CAMPBELL

47

Churches, cranes and ships. Watercolour c. 1947/8.

Wheal Jane tin mine. Oil 1949.

Boat with cat in foreground. Watercolour c. 1949.

Boats on the beach at Looe. Oil 1948.

Hayle power station and Lelant church. Oil 1948.

St Ives Bay from studio window. Oil 1950.

Halifax. Oil 1948.

London houses. Watercolour 1950.

Tuckingmill Chapel. Ink & chalk 1948.

51

The river of art and the sea
of the unconscious

In a private house in the small seaside town of Birchington in Kent is to be found a collection of the paintings of Tom Early. These range across the relatively short period of his active painting life, from 1946 to his premature death in 1967. An opportunity to re-acquaint myself with these works gives rise to many memories and unanswered questions.

I first met Tom Early in 1960. We both attended Derby College of Art and were both fortunate enough to work alongside Keith Richardson-Jones, an advocate and innovative interpreter of Basic Design, a method of education with roots in the Bauhaus and affinities to the so-called Abstract Expressionist movements on both sides of the Atlantic. St Ives was the recognised centre of this movement in Britain and it was here that Tom had begun his work, directly encouraged by Ben Nicholson. Tom made other important friendships in the Penwith Society and worked closely with them. Tom was held in some regard for this connection and the common respect and interest in such artists as Heron, Frost, Hilton, Lanyon, Mitchell and Wells, must have provided him with an ideological home-from-home on his arrival in Derby.

His integration into this scene was effortlessly managed; no polemic accompanied his settling in, he found a predetermined niche unoccupied and within a short space of time was busily engaged in his work and fully contributing to the artistic life of his new found friends. Unlike what we had come to expect from the St Ives artists of some repute, Tom's work did not comfortably conform to our expectations – his individuality set him apart. He fixed himself from the start on some remote orbit well removed from our more comfortable solar regions, where strange fruits growing as they did on alien soil and blown by inhospitable winds were not to be wondered at. Stationed thus he gave an unexpected dimension to our knowledge of what were the profitable realms of artistic activity. He was not inclined to draw us into his sphere of influence by any means beyond that of example but his steadfast position was bound to influence our ideas. It was difficult to imagine a being further out yet still engaged on a common plane of artistic endeavour.

As I sit surrounded by his paintings my attention is drawn to two works, the first called *St. Ives Bay*, 1950, and the second, *Son et Lumière*, 1963. The first work shows a maturing of his St Ives period; echoes of Ben Nicholson's earlier representational style, in his use of the Cornish landscape, are found here. *Son et Lumière* is a more independent work where any influences have been appropriated to the painter's needs and sublimated to his mature style. On closer inspection, both works betray signs of struggle with the medium. On the reverse side of the *St. Ives Bay* panel are recorded the details of one such struggle, the artist having made four attempts to complete the work in a three month period. *Son et Lumière*, for all its unified qualities, reveals on closer inspection a surface roughened by overpaintings presumably again over a prolonged period. Despite the 13 years that separate these two works they carry much the same methods of application and expressive range in the use of the medium. In both, Tom employs the widest range of manipulations of the material from thin alla prima scumblings and spare stainings to heavy encrustations, all finding their expressive purpose. Common to both are inspired passages apparently achieved with relative ease; these are neither hedonistic nor trivial, but preserved from any further modification as necessary to his vision. There is evidence that throughout his career he struggled with the medium and battled to capture the images.

In *St. Ives Bay* the recognisable elements are stirring to new possibilities, pointing towards an inner landscape, that in works such as *Son et Lumière* are more completely realised. Tom's growing facility, as shown in his later works, to navigate deeper into his psyche by the initial use of everyday experiences, illustrates the major difference between the two works. Increasingly he becomes more committed to this inner world, leaving behind only the vestigious remains of perceived reality. He is uncompromising in his search for relevant subconscious form and pays no heed to artistic niceties; however picturesque the initial experience, no trace is left by the end. It is difficult to enjoy the later works standing as they do in all their rawness and unpalatable honesty: sentinels to a singular struggle to raise flags on strange new ground.

In the earliest surviving explanation of his beliefs to Paul Hodin in 1949, Tom gives the metaphor of rivers of artistic activity all leading to a common sea of the unconscious. Whereas most artists might accept that the unconscious plays a part in the creative process it is unlikely that many would take Tom's view that this was the aim of the work. *Son et Lumière* and other later works such as the three versions of the *Lily Crucifixes*, seem to bear this out in their partially broken imagery, dissolving forms in a sea of paint barely reflecting the original likenesses. I think he was bravely prepared to risk all in this search for the internal sea.

When before his later works, I feel the need to understand them, elusive as they are, not to undo their mystery but in order to benefit from their undoubted strength.

In 1961 along with Keith Richardson-Jones, Tom founded the Derby

Group of artists, in order to give a more formal structure to the hitherto loose association of artists in the town and to bring their work to a wider audience. The inaugural exhibition was duly held at the Derby Museum and Art Gallery in April/May, 1962. What followed was a vital, if remarkable, outpouring of indignation from the citizens of the town. Letters in attack and defence peppered the pages of the *Derby Evening Telegraph* which led eventually to a demand for a meeting with the artists. The appointed evening came; the main gallery was packed with noisy members of the affronted public and on the platform among the four artist spokesmen, was Tom Early. The four faced the angry meeting. At one point they looked in danger of being swept away along with the work from the walls, but fortunately this ugly mood subsided and order was restored.

An indignant ratepayer demanded an explanation of Tom's work, work he considered his four year old capable of surpassing. There were general roars of approval. Tom's response was to stand up and face the meeting – a lone figure before a hostile sea, the room hushed in expectancy and waiting whilst Tom shifted from one foot to the other. He smiled, a warm smile, opened his mouth, only shortly after to close it again, to murmurs of impatience from the floor. Tom tried again, the room quietened; he opened his mouth for the second time but nothing came out, he smiled again and then reluctantly returned to his seat to the inevitable uproar.

No doubt there were many interested observers there that evening who would have dearly liked Tom to give them his explanations but on some occasions, and I believe this to be one of them, only time can provide such answers.

MICHAEL MILLER

In a letter dated February 11th, 1993 Mick Miller makes the following interesting comment: '. . . in his quiet way Tom was a powerful figure always seemingly on the edge but in reality in the middle!'

A portrait done from memory

Derby College of Art c. 1962. Figure Composition Class. The composition should contain a minimum of three full-length figures (with visible feet) within a perspective setting of buildings of brick or stone (including a clock-tower) and at least two trees. Predominant colours should be burnt umber and yellow ochre. Title: 'Autumn Evening'.

I'm painting quickly after coming back late from an extended lunch hour in the Regent Snooker Hall at the back of the college. The best of three frames I'd played against Dave had been delayed while we argued about whose turn it was to play the rôle of Minnesota Fats, the king of the Pittsburgh pool shooters who was dethroned by the upstart Fast Eddie Felson in the film *The Hustler* which had recently come to the local cinema and held us in its thrall. Neither of us wanted to be brash, good-looking Paul Newman. We both aspired to be honey-talking, wise old Fats, who dusted talcum powder on his pudgy hands, dabbed his dimpled chin and waddled to the table like a great big bear, then fixed Newman with his piggy little eyes and smilingly murmured, 'O.K. Fast Eddie, let's shoot some pool'.

Fats was just one of our numerous rôle models who had in common an idiosyncratic style: Mose Allison, Thelonious Monk, Bo Diddley, Nat Jackley, Edward Burra. Eccentric individuals who lived by different rules to those represented in the stifling conventions of the Figure Composition Class. None of them lived in Derby, we felt sure of that.

The door creaked open and into the room came a stooping, bearded man. Under his left arm was a brown paper parcel and in his right hand a shopping bag. Peering myopically ahead he made his way with a curious, off-balance gait to a vacant easel, sat down in front of it on a stool, unwrapped the parcel and took from it a small, half-finished canvas which he fixed to the easel after adjusting the wing-nuts until it was at the right height. All this took about half an hour. Then he carefully adjusted the spectacles on his nose and, looking just like Sigmund Freud, stared intently for a further twenty minutes at the tiny canvas. The picture consisted of a tangle of deathly white intestinal forms on a bilious, acidic green ground, above which was bare canvas and the pencilled outline of a clock tower. The combination of colour and paint texture, reminiscent of boiled tripe with mushy peas, was not one on the recommended list for Figure Comp. Indeed, the painting appeared to have no recognisable composition at all, but seemed like some nacreous, spawned thing. Weird. Interesting.

Eventually, as if waking from a dream, he unzipped the shopping bag and took from it first a palette, linseed oil and brushes, then twenty seven small tubes of oil paint which he carefully lined up side by side on the table in front of the palette. One by one he began to unscrew the tops. Twenty seven minutes later each top lay alongside its corresponding tube. He peered at them and then, once more, gazed intently at the canvas. I looked across at Dave, who had also stopped painting and was staring with bemused fascination.

The big wall clock ticked on. You could have heard a pin drop. Slowly, still staring at the canvas, he extended a hand towards a brush. The clock chimed and the class was over.

As we filed out of the room I looked back. He was carefully replacing the tops on the tubes. Outside the window the light was fading. 'An artiste', I whispered. 'Definitely,' said Dave.

IAN BREAKWELL

More private views

Keith Richardson-Jones, artist and one-time lecturer in Fine Art at Derby College of Art:

I remember Tom Early very well. We met in the days when art schools were autonomous institutions, un-attached to polytechnics or colleges of higher education; running things in ways directed to serve the interests of part-timers and mature students as well as full-time diploma students. Tom came to a weekly evening session which was also attended by some full-timers. He was always a focus of interest and curiosity. He seemed to come from somewhere else, from a world of his own devising and imagination – he was a visionary: as much a Cecil Collins as a St. Ives man – the community to which he owed his artist's origins. From St. Ives he was as much indebted to Alfred Wallis and Christopher Wood as to the Formalists, personified by his friend Denis Mitchell.

A painting by Tom Early could be mistaken for no other. Everything about it was marked by his individuality: an instinctive colour range – olive green, midnight blue, lemon yellow, linking greys, stark white, graphic black: an idiosyncratic perspective with his own rules and non-rules and impulsive expressive distortions, which on reflection put me in mind of the Abbess Hildegaard of Bingen. This leads me to recall that Tom became greatly attached to Monteverdi's Vespers during his last illness.

When I knew him during my seven years at Derby College of Art and with the short lived Derby Group, Dr. Tom Early retained links with the community psychiatric hospital, where he was highly popular with his patients who recognised his deeply humanitarian qualities. I cannot but think that his entering into imaginative rapport with the disturbed states that he would have encountered there, may well have heightened his insights, perceptions and, quite simply, his imagination.

My memory of Tom is of a highly individual artist and an extremely kind and supportive friend.

Terry Frost, artist on 'The Filter of Purity':

Tom Early and Denis Mitchell were two of the boys who were most helpful to me – particularly when they packed up one of my works – for inclusion in the exhibition at Heal's Gallery in 1951. They were two of the first artists I met who encouraged me to exhibit with them there.

Tom was a natural observer of people and places, and he didn't appear to suffer from any pressure from fashions of any kind. His memory and imagination seemed to be fitted with a filter of purity, and all his influences went through this natural selective sieve.

The particularness of his selection of colour and shapes was unique, and that strength of vision gives his work a clean and positive selection of unexpected rhythms, shapes and colours. All his looking and learning went through this process which gave his work such an individual purity of vision – the content of which is full of total honesty and love of painting.

There was a firmness that could suggest an obstinate way of seeing, and it was his way. He had a stubborn courage to do his own thing in spite of the fact that he was well aware of all the goings-on in St. Ives. A brave artist of visual honesty.

Wilhemina Barns-Graham, artist:

In a letter dated August 1993, Willie Barns-Graham remembers Tom as a 'gentle, kind and charming friend' who used to visit her studio. She recollects 'being terrified on one occasion as he insisted on carrying a bowl of boiling water off my coke stove in the Porthmeor studio over the heads of Lali Fenyvas and myself to the sink. I knew he sometimes had turns, once one in my presence – he invited me to tea at the Copper Kettle, and suddenly he gave a yell and was on the floor. People were very kind and we did what we thought was right – and I ordered a taxi and we went out to his mother at Carbis Bay. It must have been summer because I was a bit anxious and walked out to Carbis Bay to find him to my surprise standing painting at his easel! None the worse.'

About his painting she says: '. . . I think he was a beginner, and [the paintings] had a naive quality – small works, landscapes using black, yellow, green, blue on white ground and leaving in some of the white. Mostly done in oil paint, I think? His work, difficulty and inexperience perhaps with drawing, had some originality and childlike approach. But I am talking of 40 years ago, and haven't seen his work since except one at Denis Mitchell's house.

Martha Patrick, a former Courtauld Institute student, seeing Tom's paintings for the first time in 1993:

When my art teacher from school days contacted me to suggest that I go to see some of Tom Early's work, I was intrigued. More so because my art teacher had known Tom Early when he was a student and Early was living near Derby. I was also told about Tom's connection with the St. Ives Group, but little more.

Personally, I found the early works particularly appealing for their primitive quality. The views around, for example, a harbour in Cornwall in pen and ink and watercolour are unpretentious and 'childlike' in the sense of an honest kind of simplification. For me, it appears that Tom Early has seen a pattern of forms in certain views which his drawing brings out.

I looked at sketches; I noticed that his drawing was often far from assured, slick or stuck to one technique or style. He seems to have experimented a lot, not always successfully. Many sketches were what some would class as 'messy' or 'poor' drawings, but you could usually see something there that had interested Early as a note to take.

I do enjoy Early's overall use of a sombre range of colours with the odd bright colour placed effectively. Some of his narrow rectangular paintings of views in Cornwall, for example, the one from his studio window looking over the bay, are most interesting. In some of these paintings his ability to combine his imagination with a simplification and observation of the natural forms into a pattern, rhythm of colours and shapes seems quite masterly, and, although related, a great step from his earlier drawings which are more primitive in feeling.

Eve el Salahi, friend and former Slade student:

Tom's outstanding calm and benevolence was striking. He discovered an outlet for his expression in visual art. His response to the world around him seemed to be built upon his deep interest and wonderment. The marvels of nature juxtaposed against man-made chaos, jostle and commotion, all pushing into one frame, seemed to require him to stand back. Coming from the field of science and its studies of physical/human laws and behaviours, he needed to step back . . . and further back . . . to obtain a credible perspective. Aware of the gross limitations and distortions produced by human optics and brain, this distance, whilst reducing detail, revealed the patterns. This worked for Tom, and as the images merged with the artist's knowledge, his more powerful sensibilities took precedence.

Tom seemed to seek the patterns as they emerged, and which held up against the more transient relationships . . . colour, light, shape, texture. These patterns were all around . . . satisfying and constant enough, set against the everlasting space.

Laughingly toying with the fallibility of our human perception, his work seemed to challenge, as well as acknowledge, the serious study and acquired understanding drawn from the great body of scientific knowledge: but, as the images penetrated through the optics . . . permeated through the brain cells, and bounced back from the taut nerve net . . . motoring a pathway to the hand and brush . . . it seemed he was aware of the fickle nature of human interpretation, and duly allowed his strong individual sensibilities their freedom. The results promised a bonding between his awareness and life's experience.

Tom's painting represents to me his discovery of his own 'holiday haven' – a crucial discovery. Time-off from the scrutiny – the 'looking in' and 'breaking down' analysis which obsesses a huge chunk of our brain – but, rather, allowing the other chunk to live on . . . the 'looking out' mechanism. Tom's 'outlook' took the floor . . . and his 'holiday times' he shares with all who view his paintings . . . offering the key to the greatest award – integrity. This I believe, as I remember Tom.

Some public views

J.P. Hodin: 'Cornish Renaissance', *Penguin New Writing 39.*

. . . Tom Early (born 1914), who started to paint in 1946 (before that practising as a doctor), is also bewitched by the Cornish landscape. 'Any scene which has mystery appeals to me . . . Sea, cliffs, clouds; tin mines, of which there are hundreds scattered around in various states of decay, the china-clay dumps which form a landscape like that of the moon seen through a telescope.' Early is a primitivist with a freshness of approach to a motive astonishing for an intellectual who, apart from his science, has been devoted to other arts – music, poetry, the novel. I feel that the work of Alfred Wallis has given Early the courage to embark on the adventure of painting, and it may be hoped that his experiments to acquire a good painter's technique will not deprive him of his eye's talent for looking with a child's innocence upon the world in which he lives.

Michael Williams: Review of exhibition 'Fifteen Artists and Craftsmen from around St Ives', *Cornish Review*, Spring, 1951.

. . . The authentic voice of Cornwall was heard at intervals above the discipline of formal design and the clamour of colour, and nowhere more insistently than in the rapturous exclamation of Tom Early, in whose swirling panoramas the boats danced, like animated corks, in and out of the bays or lay like jazzy skeletons upon the brilliant yellow sands. In this painter and in that old magician of the Primitive, Alfred Wallis, three of whose statements of simple poetry assisted in no small measure in anchoring the exhibition to the heart of the Cornish scene, the most vibrant emotive forces were at work.

Denys Val Baker: *Britain's Art Colony by the Sea*, George Ronald, 1959.

. . . Although abstract in conception, John Wells' paintings remain full of images of Cornwall, like those of so many abstract painters who settled here. He was one of the first group of younger abstract painters associated with St Ives in the immediate postwar years; W. Barns-Graham, Patrick Heron, Bryan Wynter, Peter Lanyon, Sven Berlin, David Haughton, Denis Mitchell, Tom Early were among the others. Some, like Haughton and Early, have since left Cornwall, which is a pity, for both reflected

PAINTINGS DRAWINGS

18 - 30 July 1949

TOM
EARLY
&
DENIS
MITCHELL

Downing's Bookshop
in Fore Street
Saint Ives

Guido Morris poster for exhibition.

intensely the way in which the Cornish scene took charge of a painter's work: Haughton with his almost child's eye views of the St Just and Zennor areas, Early with his startling use of bright colours.

Tom Cross: *Painting the Warmth of the Sun: St Ives Artists 1939–1975*, Lutterworth/Alison Hodge, 1984.

... The strong flame of primitivism that burned so clearly in Alfred Wallis is also seen in the work of Tom Early who exhibited in the first of the Castle Inn exhibitions. Sven Berlin described him as 'a unique painter who leads us through landscapes of fierce intensity and terrifying loneliness without ever seeming to be aware of our dismay and our wonder at walking within a dream he has made'. The exaggerated flickering form of his painting, *Tuckingmill Chapel* has a feeling of the 'great wind' which surged through the souls of early Methodist preachers while they held their audiences in terror of hell fire, or trembling in adoration before the heavenly host.

Sven Berlin: *The Coat of Many Colours*, Redcliffe, 1994.

... Tom Early was another painter whom I have mentioned, but I cannot write further into my document of time past without recording that in him I met possibly the most fragile and sensitive but gifted person I have come upon in this strange journey. A young doctor who had been forced to give up his practice, because of the falling sickness, to find he had that rare double vision that looks through the window of the eye both ways and records the poetic image of the thing seen, empowered with the emotion and imagination coming from his lonely vision of the universe and clothing it with a strange beauty – yet seeming not to be conscious of what he had done.

Notes on a sheaf of poems by Tom Early

I think these poems are important because they are like finding a cabin door half open on the high seas where an unusual man can be seen at a kind of private meditation, which is his whole person observing and recording life as a visual artist, commenting on structure, colour, light, form, and on the human scene at each port of call, against a floating background as a ship's doctor.

For this reason I think they should be included in the composite memoir about his life and work as a painter. Like all his paintings, some of which show the influence of these observations, they are marked by a simple truth and an innocence which is starting to be licked away by the rough tongue of experience. I don't think they are great poetry, nor have pretension to be. That would spoil it. They are a unique comment on human and visual life passing through the eye and the mind of the painter before the act of art creates its own image: who knows how?

> For Art is everything, from Wrestling Jacob
> To Rembrandt's still Philosopher, in shafts of white.

Which poem to leave in or leave out, which is the modern mania for destroying the new and unknown thought that is truly creative but not immediately understood, is not for me to say, because when, without knowing, he says something profound, it is locked in by an ordinary cliché: when he is ordinary he says it in an unusual way.

In my opinion, it is best to leave them as they are, together, at the end of the book, without comment, under a separate title page: A VOYAGE TO JAPAN. This would leave the reader with much the same after-taste as when one comes out from a moving play into the busy streets of ordinary daily life and sees everything differently while driving home. That, if anything, is one of the functions of art that might be lost if they are not printed. This rare artist has been in oblivion for too long to be wasted.

SVEN BERLIN

A VOYAGE TO JAPAN

TOM EARLY

Rounding Portugal, Night

From North to South the Milky Way
Arcs overhead its silver dust;
And near we pass – a ship – an isle?
It might be either, or yet none.
Still she ploughs onwards through the seas
With magic foam, and blue for black.
Cape Finisterre is passed, tomorrow we
Shall sight the Rock. And so
With Italy to port, black Africa to starboard
The ship sails on, happily conscious not.

Mediterranean

What is it that gets one about this particular sea?
The colour, perhaps; Rome had a word for it –
"Murex" was it? – but no, there's more.
A long, sloping peninsular jutting south-east,
A land hedged in by sea-hopping enemies,
Triumphed, tho' Carthage with its fabulous elephants
Near hit the rear; but Rome beat them off.
Gradual decay from the heart set in,
At last won the battle; but still
The purple sea is there.

Port Said

A dun-coloured stage set for actors to play on,
And play they do; thronging the boat
Almost before she has anchored; "Buy this, missee –
See here, cheep cheep" says the gouly-gouly man
With chick in either hand. Now Farouk's gone,
But the party on nearby destroyer's not gone
Till early morn leave ashes of dead wine.
Menacing opening to Canal, even the trees look fake here;
Perhaps they are.

Suez Canal

Afar, a barren horizon; by the wave-lapped shore
Bushlets of scrub grow, here a delicious island
Outstuck toward ship, with palm and pine tree
Surrounding its delicate filigree huts.
The children bathe in droves, shrieking for joy
And again the barren horizon.
For the eye sees not the scarring diseases,
Beggars sitting squat, cross-legged,
The children blind from birth, for whom Tintoretto
Not even a name. And round all the level horizon.

Red Sea: Night

No stars to sing their lucid, uncomplaining song
Only the foam of the ship's wake, cream-white;
And the temperature falls to 90, and we sigh
Relief for the 100 it had been.
The engines throb day-in, night-out
And men in white walk round their duty.
The thankless task of seeing one more ship
Sail from cool London, through sticky heat
Of the Red Sea, to Aden and the East.

Aden

A jagged topline shows, rather like Skye
And below the houses are yellow.
Yellow, with pink roofs; and here a strange mosque,
A touch of white in some of the squarer houses
And always the grey rock, like mine castings
In Stoke-on-Trent. The monsoon winds
Are cooler than Red Sea stagnation.
A faded, rather jaded, rock one feels
Which history somehow seems to have missed,
Though point of touch to India and the East
Since Canal opened to strains of Aida.

Indian Ocean: Monsoon

Aye, but she's bucking now, the great sea-horse,
Riding the waves and giving foam for spray
Which tops the decks. Better
This movement is than Red Sea heat
Though lunch time sees the empty places,
And visions come of pinched, sad faces
Making their peace with God, alone in cabins.
Sway as we do, One leads towards the shudder
And there must come the full-stop, Nature's rudder.

'Lavengro' in the Indian Ocean

It was Borrow that kept me up reading one night,
Though the swell was spilling the soup-plates around
And pitching the tea cups. To starboard
A strange wintry moon in that hot climate
Lit up for us the island of Socotra;
But still I was reading George Borrow, entranced
Like the snakes in his story.
There was Borrow on Failure – and I remembered
How Peter Warlock had sent these lines to his friends
When they were downcast: 'Thou wouldst be joyous,
Wouldst thou? Then be a fool.
What great work was ever the result
Of joy, the puny one?' Yet this book seemed to me
Of all books the most joyous.

Why Write Poetry?

Why should one bother oneself with poetry? Why indeed
When there is so much poverty and all the need.
It is because one must – it comes in a flash,
And one reaches for things to write down, in a dash;
It is all there, and must be pulled out in a passion
If I am not to follow the last man's fashion.
It is a struggle, and of all people
None knew it better than Constable, painting Salisbury steeple.
Music, painting, poetry – all art is a fight
And comes with sense of knowing it so, just right.

Clouds, Evening

Through Westering clouds dissolving, a pearl-grey sun
Shines feebly; and shapes from the dark
Take form, and melt; Rubens's monkey is there
Along with Michaelangelo's blustering Breather of Life.
But already the whole design's breaking down,
Or building up fearful Turner-like rockscapes.
Yet skywards it is men look for all that's stable;
Down here things lurch, slide, crash into a table.

71

Moonlight

Moon's South-East now; and the boiling scum
Seems to draw onward toward the rising sun.
Ship sailing calm this night, without a swell;
Though how much longer who can tell?
Soon we shall try to fix ourselves again,
As the sad ocean turns into an ocean-pain.
After Penang the islands, and we wish
For smoother travel, not to feed the fish.

Occupational Complaint

Whate'er the weather, doctor remains on 's pins
Can only think about some past, sad sins.
For it never pours but it rains, as B– once joked
And day for needle-pricks is spoked
By engineer gashing his arm, needing stitches.
Is it small wonder that the doctor twitches
At end of day, all in, for two small drinks?
Then gratefully into his bunk he sinks.
Oh! for some fine, small restful illness;
Only the memories of Handel and Sibelius
Keep him from being a real old table-cuss.

Port Swettenham

And sweat – 'em too she does, this drab old port
Out of low trees and islands wrought.
Curious Diesel from Stafford, with plungers on wheels
Picks up the dove-grey, steel-white trucks and reels
Back to the station. For this is warring Malay,
And trucks are armoured cars 'gainst hold-up or foray.
Only one crimson gate gives spark of life in dead
Grey rows of tin-plate shed.
Even the circling, moth-eaten crows are grey,
Looking like Gordon's Khartoum vultures at prey.
Abstract air of unimportance lies over this place,
An air exactly still, heat-hitting in face.

Hong Kong

A peak, the clouds rising like mist above rain,
And cooler than blood-heat of yesterday.
Green cliffscape on entry rather like Cornwall;
With red rock added,
But no more of Devon.
Here a delicate, aluminium-silvered Pagoda
But down by the water front ugly
Slabs of building in ochre.
People swarm the boat more than is usual,
And rain douses all.

Taku-bar (North China)

We arrived at Taku expecting all incivility,
And received instead all politeness.
The ancient Chinese grace overcame Marxist inhumanity
As it has risen above dogma throughout history.
Short crossing to a happy land of islands, Japan;
But East faces East over the narrow sea.
Why this absurd stalemate, brought on
By a few hard-faced men of politics?
Half the world starves in small lands in the East, yet
We waste our substance in war. We deserve to perish.

Japan - 1. Industrial

London rush-hour, in some vast Metropolis
Embracing Tokyo and Yokohama in one,
And the men coatless in white shirts.
Strange tragedy this, beginning with Commodore Perry's
Opening of Japanese trade to the West in 'eighteen-fifties,
And the last scene – war.
The further tragedy of Americanisation of Tokyo,
But prime cause the too sudden
Impact of West on Japan in a century,
Overnight change from a pastoral to electric age.
Endless wires stretching out far from city,
Ugliest imitations of bankers' buildings in centre;
But the poverty-stricken shacks remain.

Japan - 2. Rural

Pink Fujiyama, etched-out eerily by moonlight
Or sunset lighting its cloud-capped crater with orange.
Mist-shrouded, angular foreground of mountains
Covered by patchwork fields, criss-cross; and fir trees.
Not much sign here of spurred-on industry
Though by the water-front a few oil cylinders,
And an occasional chimney.
By the shrines of ancient town, the devotees
Still doff their shoes to the fierce-faced god of war,
With his sheath of arrows.
But the people are easy, and no wonder
They call the silent volcano sacred.

Japan - 3. People

Somehow the people fit the landscape in charm,
They have that mystery and sweetness a waterfall has;
Something too of its ferocity.
Even in the brash screechings of electric trains
They manage to look detached and unconcerned.
But the children! Brown, naked nymphs when bathing,
They are entirely delightful.
In this land of great contrasts, of mountains rising
From the very doorsteps of harsh cities,
The people too vary greatly
In different places, but are always
Friendly and talkful, though East and West separate sorely;
But the look and the handclasp cure all.

75

Farewell Japan

A bright sunset in crimson and gold
Stood out as we edged our way between islands,
To the open sea.
How sad we were to be leaving this land
Of the cherry blossom and the rising sun,
And the noisy trams with their peculiar hooters;
Of sudden downpours in torrential fierceness,
And the ever-lovely mountains and trees.
But most of all because of the people
With their time-old Eastern friendliness,
Grace, and beauty; how they will be missed!

The Summing-up (Mediterranean)

The sea's a battleground, of that one grows
More certain as each evening glows.
Men against steel: steel against salt,
The fight's more unremitting with each halt.
Now as we hit once more the Med.,
And leave behind with relish the sea called Red
I must make summing, for as Auden said:
    'To set in order – that's the task
    Both Eros and Apollo ask.'

I wander round the decks, and wand'ring wonder
If any wreckage last us from Jove's thunder.
This ship, now: steady progress mostly
With an odd, rather ghastly, ghostly
Reminder that the deeps are all too deep,
More so than Everest; and one has a peep
At ships torpedoed ten – twelve – years ago,
Hanging in depths which might be topped by snow.
The gallant convoys of those hideous years
Grow dim again; and still one fears
That memories, fading to even as dim
Will less than justice do to those within;
A motley crew, no doubt, whose bones grow cold
But to the bravest yet they match, these bold.
Sailors they were, and on what fretful sea?
We shall meet others in the come-to-be.

76

Now different thoughts come scrambling up for air,
Like depth-charged U-boats crew, they wonder where.
Man's life is short, his destiny is hidden –
Who can say other, watching fever-ridden
Tribes of the Eastern sky, of Africa, the Indies?
All one can think: our future's dark and misty.
But clouds break out, and fitfully gleams the sun
When here the infamous spirochaete is done
To dissolution by the work of one;
And yaws and tubercle, the double curses,
At least a link there, breaking Hell's twin nurses.

Now ship sails close by land of Art's own womb,
Italy, and twinkling lights all round no room
Allow of narrow straits; but they are there,
And through Messina lumbers like a bear.
For Art is everything, from Wrestling Jacob
To Rembrandt's still Philosopher, in shafts of white;
And Brahms and Toscanini both together raise
A shout of joy which is much more than praise.
From Dante to old Verdi, score on score
Saw life and death within this narrow shore;
And wonder not, the impulse which broke out
When sunsets, seen from Tuscany a rout
Of colour; crimson, yellow-pale, all fixed
By grey-dark mass of clouds, unmixed.
How could this fail to turn the men
To paint their olive groves, and then
Create the domes of Florence – Venice stone,
With bronzen horses – oldest yet, old Rome.

But give us time! The race is not yet run,
And England far from sunk beneath the sun.
For Britain stands, as stood alone in 'forty
Not vicious, kind; both tolerant and naughty.
Shall we survive? A world stands poised in breath
Waiting to know the choice 'twixt life and death.
And choose we must; an infinite outstretching life,
Or its extinction on this planet, cut-like knife.
Behind Genoa the hills loom up from sea,
Granting assurance; but it may not be:
Although this ancient, lovely town says Yes
Many there are who wear a stranger's dress.
Our fate's not pre-ordained, we can think twice and mend;
If not we're sunk, or well around the bend.

Somerset Churches

Gracious as lace,
In fact laceous, not grace-
ous should be the word.
By hill or in valley
They stand, tree-topped
As the sad sun stops.
The train passes Bruton,
Cricketers standing, white on green
'Tween the church and the track.
How unlike these churches are
From those of Devon,
Squarer though gracious still;
And Cornwall; where as Auden saw
The granite resists the sea
And our type of thinking ends.
Here fierce square granite churches
Do indeed resist the sea.
Beauty's not the right word, I suppose
For these gaunt towers on moorland;
But they grip the heart more
Than proud charmers of Somerset.

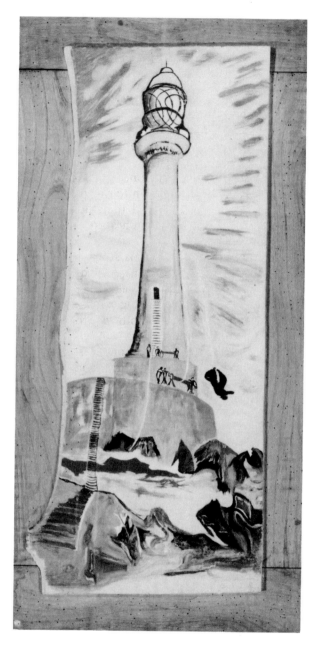

Relief of Bishop Rock lighthouse. Oil 1949.